LOVELY THINGS IN UGLY PLACES

by Mattie Montgomery

Table of Contents

Introduction

I think God loves the broken ones. Maybe that's my youthful zeal or relentless naïveté speaking, but I *actually* believe that there is a special place in God's heart for those who are forgotten or feared by most of our post-modern church.

Over the last decade, I have spent many of my nights in smoky bars, sharing awkward moments with people who have given up on faith, and who doubt—sometimes violently—the existence of a loving God. During that time, I beheld time and time again a truth that transcended my understanding and whispered to my heart during the many moments that left me speechless: *Wherever fear has built a wall, love can build a bridge.* Even in the ugliest places, the light of hope can shine into the darkness of despair. And if we're willing to step bravely in to the cold emptiness that so many call life, we just might see the beauty of hope begin to blossom again where there was once nothing.

As I write this, I am sitting on a tour bus in Dessau, Germany, getting ready to play another concert with my band *For Today*. A girl with blue hair just walked by the window, smoking a cigarette and holding hands with a guy who has a star tattooed on his face. This is my tribe. Most of us are awkward and antisocial; sometimes we're angry, sometimes we're sad, but at the end of the day, we're glad to have each other. Metal heads need love too (no matter how hard we try to pretend we don't).

Tonight, I will stand on stage at a metal show in a bar, and talk about Jesus to a crowd of people, most of whom just showed up to get drunk and crowd surf. Some of them will roll their eyes and laugh at me for it. Some of them will get angry and give me the finger for it. And some of them will have their lives changed forever. That's just the way it goes here. I learned long ago that I can't make people believe anything. No matter how persuasive or passionate I try to be, people only find what they are looking for. And tonight— just like the thousands of other times I have taken the stage in venues just like this around the world—I am looking for those who are looking for hope.

I am a different man today than I was the first time I stepped on stage. A lot has happened over the years I've spent on the road with this band. Some of it has been beautiful and some of it has been devastating, but even if I could, I wouldn't change a thing. It has been, after all, the times of greatest trial that taught me both who I am, and who I want to be.

Before we go any further, I feel like I should tell you up front, I am *not* the hero of this story. Most of the time, I felt more like a passive bystander—a happenstance onlooker witnessing these transformative moments in people's lives and feeling overwhelmed at how strangely sweet or painfully sorrowful these moments can be. I've been blessed to see the hand of God working silently in the hearts and minds of men, molding them patiently and tenderly into the likeness of the person He wants them to be.

So what I'm writing here is not a book about God or religion; and it's not really a book about me either. This is the story of a few

3

silly kids who were fortunate enough to bump into each other during our desperate search for purpose. This is the story of what can happen when we are crazy enough to actually take God at His word. *We* have not been perfect, but we are living proof that *He* has been and continues to be. In both our successes and failures, through our victories and defeats, we have learned enough to know that we know very little, and we have grown enough to be okay with that.

This is the story of a wild adventure that I was dragged into nearly ten years ago. It has lead me all over the world, put my life on display in front of millions of people, and has been a constant reminder of just how small I really am. If I'm totally honest with you, I'm really not cut out for this. I never was. But I was ambitious (or maybe naïve) enough to say "yes" to it anyway.

In writing this book, my desire is to take you with me as I relive some of the most significant moments of this journey, and to show you the things I've encountered along the way that have been so pivotal in making me me. I want you to see the beautiful hope that is born in the most pitiful circumstances, the resilience of the

human heart, and the power of perfect love to conquer even the

deepest fear. I truly hope that, in reading these stories of

impossible things that have happened to (and sometimes *because

of*) ordinary people, you might find the courage to believe that, as

you dare to look, you too can find *lovely things in ugly places.*

Chapter 1

GOD TOLD ME

The smoke hurt my eyes. I was drenched in sweat and out of breath as I walked off the little stage in a dark corner of Mac's Bar in Lansing, Michigan. "This will be my last show as the vocalist of *Besieged*," I had just told the crowd. "It's been incredible, but tomorrow, I'll be hitch-hiking to Iowa to join a band called *For Today*."

Nobody knew who *For Today* was. And, to be honest, I don't think most of them really cared. Most of them were more concerned with nursing their cigarettes and meeting up with their friends than they were with the band violently clamoring away in the corner, but this moment was destiny for me. A lot had happened to bring me to this point. Just a few months prior, I had decided I wanted to try to follow Jesus. But as it turns out, that is much easier said than done. I had tried and failed more times than I could count to convince my friends that I didn't want to live the same life I used to live. But no matter how hard I tried, I found myself spending time with the *same* friends and going to the *same* parties. Those *same* behaviors were only getting me the *same* results as before.

I needed a new environment. I needed to *go*. I didn't care where, or really with whom, I just knew I needed to *go*—to travel, and to see this world I had dreams of changing. The other members of *Besieged* had no desire at all to *go* anywhere, and the only thing I was really good at was screaming. (Yeah. Screaming. That's a real talent that real people really have.) So one day, a friend of mine called to tell me there was this band from Iowa called *For Today* that was looking for a vocalist. I'd never met the guys in the band before, and I'd never been to Iowa before, but my friend assured me of two things: First, these guys loved God; and second, they had plans to *go*. I was sold.

In September of 2007, after connecting with *For Today*, and informing the members of *Besieged* of my plan to leave the band and head to Iowa after our concert in Lansing, I set the plan in motion. I packed my bags and headed to the concert, planning to play the show, sleep on a park bench, then hitch-hike to Iowa the next morning (desperate times call for desperate measures...). After making my announcement to the crowd, I walked off stage smelling like a cross between an ashtray and an armpit, and I found a girl named Anna waiting for me.

I had met Anna before, and she had become a friend. Anna is a tall girl, with short, brown hair, thick, square-framed glasses, and a beige cardigan. She looked like somebody's mom who was supposed to just drop them off at the show, but decided to stay and check it out. Or maybe like some kind of heavy metal librarian. I liked Anna.

"Can we talk outside for a minute?" she asked.

"Of course," I replied, "Let's go!"

We walked out of the side door of the dirty venue and down the metal staircase to the parking lot. She stopped abruptly, reaching deep into to the pocket of her sweater. She looked up at me and said, "I feel like God told me to give you this." Her hand opened to reveal a stack of $20 bills. "Its two hundred dollars," she said. "Maybe you can use this to buy a bus ticket so you won't have to hitch-hike."

I'd never met anyone before that could say that God has actually *talked* to them. I stumbled over my words. "Wow... I mean... Thank you so much!" I managed to piece together. "You really don't have to do this."

"I want to," she assured me.

"Well then, okay! I sure won't stop you," I replied with a chuckle, as she dropped the cash into my hand.

She gave me a hug and left me with, "I really think God has great things for you." Somehow, I *believed* her.

That night, as I tossed and turned, thinking about what the next day would mean for the rest of my life, I kept coming back to what Anna had said: "I feel like God told me to give you this." God *told* her to? What does that even mean? How did she know it was

God? And, if God sent this girl to give me $200 so I could get to Iowa, He must *really* want me to join *For Today*! Right?

I woke up with the sun the next morning and had a friend drive me to the Greyhound station in Lansing. I walked up to the desk and bought a one-way ticket from Lansing, Michigan to Sioux City, Iowa.

Little did I know, that was the moment everything changed.

God had gotten involved.

THE TEAM

The next day, on a sunny September morning, after 12 hours folded up uncomfortably and trying in vain to sleep in my tiny Greyhound bus seat, we finally pulled into Sioux City. I disembarked, and with the faint smell of garbage and sewer pizza filling my nostrils, I anxiously surveyed what I thought would be the starting point for the rest of my life.

Sioux City, Iowa is a really stinky place. They built a dog food factory and a chicken processing plant right next to the interstate—

it does *not* make for a good first impression! But my optimism endured. I pulled my shirt up over my nose and headed for the sidewalk where the band was waiting for me.

Our meeting was mostly awkward hugs and handshakes with David, the drummer, and Brandon, the bass player.

David was a small guy, with short, brown hair, one crooked tooth and cool-guy sideburns. He was the brains of the operation; he handled all the band business with ease and excellence, and even found time to make extra money from whatever internet scheme was popular at the moment.

Brandon looked like he was *almost* 12 years old, and seemed like the kind of kid that would remind you of that fact if you ever called him "only" 11 (I think he was actually 16 at the time). He weighed probably just over 100 pounds, and had the physique of an old greyhound dog, a fact accentuated by his extra-small t-shirt. He was also wearing slippers. Not because he had forgotten to put on his real shoes; no, the slippers were the only shoes he owned. They were comfortable, he said, and he had no plans to step in water, so they would suit him just fine.

The three of us stopped to eat tacos at La Juanita, the best restaurant in Sioux City, then headed over to the church they had been using as a practice space to wait for the other two members to arrive. The church had soft pink carpet along the floor that matched the padding on the pews, and potted plastic flowers lined the building. It was the least hardcore place I've ever been. After a few minutes, Brandon's older brother, Ryan walked in with his guitar case in hand. He was a little intimidating (to be honest, I've known Ryan for almost 10 years now, and I'm *still* kind of intimidated by him…).

His long brown hair curled around the bottom of his all black Braves baseball cap, the brim of which cast a shadow over his light blue eyes. He wore a stern expression like he had just had a troubling realization and was about to voice his concern. Nothing was troubling him, though, and he wasn't about to voice a concern about anything, that's just how his face looks. Ryan wrote all the

13

music for the band, and had a tattoo on his shoulder that was only visible because he had cut the sleeves off his t-shirt. He was very cool. After greeting me, he went to work setting up his giant wall of amps and speakers – a whole realm of things I have never understood. Watching him, I thought he might be a genius, and I was glad he was on my team.

Lastly, about a half hour late, the door opened and in walked the band member I would eventually grow closest to, Mike. Mike had shaggy, dirty blonde hair and the beginnings of an awesome beard. He dressed more like a surfer than a metal head, and had a big smile on his face. He took a few steps into the room, then stopped suddenly, squinted his eyes at me, and whispered loudly to the rest of the guys, "Uh...you didn't tell me he was *black!*"

Awkward silence.

After a few seconds of quiet, wide-eyed terror from the rest of the band, Mike erupted with laughter at his own joke and broke the tension for the rest of us. "I'm totally kidding," he assured me

14

as he wrapped me up in a big hug like I was his long lost brother. "I only had one chance to get you with that one and I didn't want to miss it!"

"Well, that's what I get for being black, I guess," I said sarcastically. I knew immediately that Mike had no interest in formalities and I liked that. He was my favorite.

After spending about an hour running through songs at rehearsal, we set down the instruments and pulled some chairs together from the back row of the church. We talked about our weaknesses and fears, confessed our struggles, studied scripture, and prayed for each other.

That was when I knew this was really going to work. This group was different.

One moment from that day has stayed with me through the years since. During the course of the conversation, I turned to Mike and said, "Let's preach the gospel until Jesus comes back, or they kill us for it, whichever comes first." He agreed emphatically, we shook hands, and just like that, our minds were made up: We would be given fully to the call of ministry—even if our ministry would look very different than anything we had ever seen before.

DAY ONE – TOUR

The cold, dry air of an early Iowa morning filled our lungs. Our sleeping bags were stuffed under the seats in our big, purple, soccer-mom van, and we climbed in full of excitement and enthusiasm. We had rehearsed hard for the last week to prepare for this, the first of 60 straight days of tour. We were a real band (whatever that is), leaving on a real tour, to play our music for real fans. We drove a few hours to the first show, scheduled in the small town of Buffalo, Minnesota, buzzing like little boys on Christmas morning.

We performed that night like we were in Wembley Stadium. We weren't. It wasn't a big show, but it was a big moment for us. It felt like we had finally stepped into the thing we were made to do. It's a feeling I have only had a few times in life—it's something I will never forget.

After the concert that night, while mingling with the crowd and meeting the people that had come to see us, I met Jacob. Jacob was an olive-skinned skater kid with shaggy hair who was from Minneapolis. He came to the concert because he loved heavy metal music and hated being at home. Jacob didn't have a dad and his mom was an addict. He came to concerts with his friends looking for a place to belong. When he pushed his way through the crowded room to come talk to me about how much he loved the concert, I remembered the commitment I had made to Mike just a few days earlier, mustered all my courage, and awkwardly asked the question I would go on to ask thousands of other people over the years: "Do you know Jesus?"

Jacob answered enthusiastically, "I've been to church with my friends a couple times!"

"That's good, man. But do you KNOW Jesus? He's alive!" I continued. "And, the first time I ever felt His presence, it changed my life forever!"

Jacob scrunched his eyebrows together and shrugged his shoulders. "I mean, I've heard about Him before..."

I was excited now. I had lived a lot of my life feeling exactly like Jacob. Growing up, I knew *about* Jesus. I even knew *a lot* about Jesus, but I hadn't really known *Him.* I knew first-hand the frustration and confusion that can come from hearing stories about what God has done for other people; I had spent years wondering why I wasn't special or significant enough to get His attention. That night, I needed to share with Jacob the thing I had just learned myself—that we already *have* God's attention.

"Let's go outside and talk," I suggested.

Jacob eagerly agreed and we pushed our way through the post-concert chaos, out the back door, and into the alley behind the venue. Once outside, I shared my story with him. Then I shared *his* story with him.

"God *loves* you, Jacob. And, it would be a tragic thing for you live your life hearing *about* that love, but never experiencing it for yourself."

18

I ended with, "Would you like to maybe pray, and start a real relationship with Him tonight?"

Without hesitation, Jacob nodded his head yes, his eyes filled with tears. "I really want to know God," he said. "I *need* Him."

So there, next to a dumpster in the back alley of a small venue, after a heavy metal concert in Buffalo, Minnesota, I stood with young Jacob—the son of an absentee father and a drug addict mother—and listened to him talk to the God of the universe for the first time in his life. He asked God to forgive him for his sins, and he asked God to give him a new life, one full of hope and purpose. At one point in his prayer he said the f-word. Jacob didn't know how to pray right, but I don't think God cared at all.

I haven't spoken with Jacob in years, but I know one thing about that night: *I* have never been the same.

I was hooked. I had found my purpose. If our band never made any money, if we never got to travel the world, or make music videos, or ride in a big tour bus, all those nevers would be no sacrifice at all if we were able to see more people like Jacob find hope in our message. That day, I forgot all about building our band, and I got obsessed with building His kingdom.

I learned a beautiful truth on day one of our first tour—that real joy would never be found on the platform of fame, but in the trenches of ministry. I found out that, despite what I'd seen in church as a kid or on Christian TV, God is not impressed by the extravagance of our buildings or the price of our clothes, He is moved by humble authenticity. The God I saw that day is willing to meet skater kids in alleyways. He answers prayers with the f-word in them.

Maybe God wasn't as uptight as I had always imagined. That was an exciting thought.

And He was just getting started.

Chapter 2

GROWING TOGETHER

We hit the road hard. We played seven shows a week, every week, for two months straight, and we loved it. It was like a self-funding road trip with all our best friends. The concerts weren't big— sometimes we played in the basement of someone's house, sometimes we played in barns or skate parks. We weren't rock stars. We were just kids playing music we liked with people we loved. (To be honest, that's *still* what we are. Only now, more people are listening.)

Each day, we would all come together at some point and one of us would share what we had learned from our personal time in scripture, then we would pray for each other and for the kids that were going to come to the concert that night. Doing this every day seemed so innocent and simple to us at the time. It wasn't some profound or admirable discipline we had adopted, we just liked to talk about Jesus. It's funny though, now, as I think back to our daily time in the Word, fellowship, and prayer, I am more convinced than ever that these were the things that carried us through the pressures and pitfalls of success in such an ugly industry.

As we came together as brothers and sloppily stumbled around the things we thought we understood from the Bible, we were inadvertently building a foundation that has remained strong for us through the years. The lessons we learned in that time were lessons that would give shape to our ministry, our music, our marriages, and our lives. In these little meetings in our purple soccer-mom van, we defined who we wanted to be as men, and each of us discovered a unique identity that would stay with us forever.

TWO PEOPLE

After a few weeks of this, we pulled into San Antonio, Texas, for a concert we had scheduled there. We'd never been to San Antonio before, and we were excited about the opportunity. Eventually, the doors opened and some of the other bands started playing. Someone went inside to scope out the crowd, and brought back some interesting news.

"Guess how many people there are in there!"

"How many?"

"Two."

"Two?"

"Yep. Two."

Turns out, San Antonio didn't care about *For Today*. A whopping crowd of *two whole people* had come out to see our band play that night. As we discussed our humbling predicament, someone suggested that we maybe wouldn't need to bring in *all* our equipment. I mean, we had lights, and speakers, and amps, and things that were really just for show. And they were all pretty heavy, so none of us really liked carrying them. Also, let's be honest…no matter how good our show was that night, impressing these *two people* wasn't going to make or break our career.

As we continued to discuss, Mike posed a question that stopped us all in our tracks. "Do we do this for people, or do we do this for God?"

That simplified the situation.

"We do this for God," I replied. "So let's give Him our absolute best."

Everyone else nodded their approval, and we went to work, unloading *all* our equipment into the venue.

Things changed a bit after that. We adopted a new philosophy that day. We decided that in every situation, whether people noticed or not, we would do our best. This was not an idea born of business strategy or musical passion, but out of one simple thought: Even if *nobody* else was there to watch our band, God was. And we refused to give Him anything less than our very best efforts with the talents He gave us.

We played the show that night, and we gave it our all. It was every bit as awkward as you can imagine – probably more so. But the thing I remember most about that night is this: We played our hearts out in front of *two people*. And, that night, in San Antonio, Texas, there were *two people* who made decisions to follow Christ.

I saw a fundamental truth played out in front of my eyes that night. As we are faithful with the "little" things, we position ourselves for more. Everyone wants to be a rock star who gets to play their heart out in front of tens-of-thousands of screaming fans. Thank God, we didn't get to *that* point without first playing our hearts out in front of two indifferent bystanders. We are better for the slow path we traveled. We have had many other underwhelming concerts since that day, but it was during the awkward, humbling days of our early career that God worked in us the character and the perspective necessary to be able to handle the tremendous responsibility He has entrusted us with since then.

So, to those of you reading this who desire to someday hold a place of great influence—whether in business, ministry, music, or anything else—don't despise the process. And carry this truth with you wherever you go: It is only by giving our best today that we build our best tomorrow.

THE GIRL

One night, toward the end of 2007, we drove from a concert in Hot Springs, Arkansas, to McCalla, Alabama—a small town just outside of Birmingham. When we arrived at about dawn, the owner of the venue came by and let us in so we could get some sleep before the concert. We stumbled in the door with drooping eyes and bad breath and flopped down on their couches to go right back to sleep. This show was going to be a special one, as we were booked to open the concert for three other bands that were much bigger than us.

It was a bright, warm December morning in Alabama. As a kid from Michigan, "warm December morning," was something I had never experienced before, so I got up a couple hours earlier than the rest of the guys and went for a walk outside. I carried my Bible with me with thoughts of what I might share at our next Bible study.

I spent some time walking, some time reading, and some time praying—just enjoying the morning and quietly acknowledging

26

God. After a while, as I meandered aimlessly back across the parking lot, a faint flicker of light on the ground caught my eye. I looked and saw a ring lying on the concrete. It looked like it might be white gold, and it had eight small stones sparkling in a line across the top. It was too small to fit me (I'm clearly *far* too manly to ever wear something like that anyway...), but it was beautiful, too beautiful for me to just throw it back on the ground. I dropped it into my pocket, assuming I'd figure out what to do with it later.

As the rest of the band members began to wake up and poke their heads out of their holes, we planned out and began our day. We went to find lunch. The other bands arrived with friendly hugs and high fives, and unloaded all their equipment. We organized our gear on the stage and ran through a sound check in preparation for the show. We all went out to dinner as a crowd of over 400 people shuffled in through the double doors in the front of the building. We played our set. I preached the Gospel. And I forgot all about the ring in my pocket.

Hours later, at the very end of the night, I was standing in the back of the room, meeting show-goers and thanking them for coming. While talking with a friend, I casually stuck my hands in my pockets, and my finger brushed against the smooth curve of the ring. I grasped it between two fingers and pulled it out, remembering my thought to "figure out what to do with it later." It was "later" now, and I still had no idea what to do with it. As I lifted my head, I saw two girls walking up to chat with us, so I held my hand out, with the ring in the middle of my palm, and said to one of them as they got close enough to hear me, "Here, this is for you!"

"Really?" she replied, caught off guard.

"Yep!" I said, nodding my head. "I found it on the ground earlier and I don't know what to do with it."

She took it from my hand and slipped it onto her ring finger. "It fits perfectly!" She exclaimed. "I guess that means we're supposed to get married now."

"I guess so," I said, joining in with her sarcasm.

Now, I feel like I should describe this girl to you. She was small. (When I say "small," I don't mean that she was a child, I mean she was just a very small person. Not like a dwarf or anything, just smaller than regular people. I should stop now before this gets any more out of hand. I'm so sorry if I've offended anyone...) What I'm trying to say is, she was less than five feet tall, and weighed *maybe* 100 lbs. She had long, brown hair, tied back with a polka-dotted headband like a little gypsy woman, tan skin, and beautiful, dark hazel eyes that you would only know were hazel if you looked really hard.

I knew. I was looking really hard.

"But my dad would kill me if I brought home a black boy," she continued.

"Oh... Uh... Well...that's ok. I'm not really trying to get you to bring me home," I replied, having just been awkwardly introduced to the reality of an Alabama I'd only read about in books. "Which band did you come to see tonight?" I asked, scrambling to steer the conversation away from marriage, or racism, or dads, or murder.

29

"No one, really," she said. "We just came to talk with some of these girls about Jesus."

"Really?"

"Yeah. You see, before I met Him, I used to get drunk and come to concerts like this, looking for a place to fit in. So now, I thought this might be a good place for me to help some of the girls that are in the same spot I used to be in."

"That's incredible!" I replied. "What's your name?"

"I'm Candice," she said in a voice musical with a soft southern accent.

"I'm Mattie," I held out my hand to shake hers. "Nice to meet you."

And with that, I had met the girl I would spend the rest of my life with. It took some time for us to figure it out, but our awkward "Hey, here's a ring," "OMG it fits perfectly, we're supposed to get married. Too bad you're black," exchange is something that will be a part of our story forever. Her dad doesn't hate me. To be honest, I'm not sure he even realizes that I'm black.

She still has the ring I gave her the day we met. It's pretty beat up

now; the shine has gone out of it and a few of the stones have

fallen out, but it hangs on her key ring just inside the door of our

house. It did its job well and I'm grateful.

Of all the days I could have found a ring on the ground, it

had to be that one. Of all the moments throughout the day in which

I could have pulled the ring out of my pocket, it *had* to be that one.

Of the 400 people in attendance that day, it *had* to be her who

walked up to me as I stood there with the ring in my hand. And, of

all the girls in the world, I *had* to be hers. That was the first day of

the wildest adventure I will ever be a part of.

This brown-haired girl from Birmingham, Alabama, would

teach me to love, challenge me to grow, and become the mirror in

which I am able to see my strengths and weaknesses. And it all

started with a ring.

THAT TIME I MET JESUS

Days passed and turned into weeks, weeks turned into months. Candice and I kept in touch but never really got to see each other. I was in a different city every night, and only near Alabama every few months. I once heard a friend say about marriage, "When it's right, it's right." And I knew it was right for me to be with this girl. She made me better (she still does), so we would find a way to make it work, even though we both knew that would mean waiting.

Later that year, out on the road in Indiana, we band members slept on the floor of Donita's house. Donita was a wild lady. Her kids loved *For Today*, and she loved her kids, so we were always welcome at her place. We stayed there many times when we came through their area, and she was always very gracious and hospitable to us. She was a mama to many, our band included.

One morning, after having slept on the floor in Donita's living room with the rest of the band, I woke up to the sound of her shuffling around the house, collecting her things and getting ready to leave. She saw me awake and said, "I'm going to go soak. Would you like to come?"

"I...don't know what that means," I replied, rubbing the sleep from my eyes.

She laughed and said, "I'm just going to go over to our church and turn on some worship music. It's something I like to do to just spend time with God."

It seemed harmless enough to me, so I agreed. "Let's do it!"

We got into her car and made the short drive to her church. It was one of those weird churches—dimly lit, shofars and bottles of anointing oil everywhere, purple flags hanging on the walls... I loved it! We walked into the sanctuary and she went straight to the soundboard saying she would turn on some music.

If I'm honest, I think the word "music" was a stretch. What Donita turned on was just...very terrible. I mean, it was a recording of some guy who was *clearly* making up the words to his song as he went along, and on top of that, he was not a good singer—not at all! I think God liked it anyway.

There I sat in my seat, regretting my decision to come "soak" with Donita. She didn't miss a beat though. It only took her about 30 seconds to kick her shoes off and start pacing back and forth on the side of the room. She waved her arms around and sang and prayed loudly.

Donita was a Pentecostal powerhouse, and I was sitting there thinking back to that one time I closed my eyes during a worship song. I was *way* out of my league.

But there, with my hands folded uncomfortably in my lap, sitting in the middle of Donita's charismatic church for crazy Christians, I closed my eyes again. Words popped into my head. "Seek my face," they said. I had heard that phrase before, probably in some church service or Christian book. I didn't really know what it meant, but I assumed it was what God said to someone in Bible times when He wanted them to come hang out. So, I thought, *God, I want to seek your face!* I didn't know how to do that, or what it might entail, but I thought, *If God wants to spend time with people, then I want to be one of those people!*

So I let out a sigh and said under my breath, "Okay." Then I squeezed my eyes closed, scrunched up my nose, gritted my teeth, and thought, *This is it! I'm seeking His face! Here we goooooooooooo...!*

Nothing.

I don't know what I expected really—maybe an earthquake or a beam of light from heaven. But what I *got* was nothing. I was still sitting in that dumb church listening to that dumb music with dumb Donita. I'm not sure if I got humble or I got desperate, but after a few minutes I decided to try again. This time I would cut the fanfare and just be honest with God.

God, here I am. If you'll have me, I just want to be with you today.

A deep breath.

I had had moments with God before, but I don't know that God had ever really had a moment with *me*.

Another deep breath.

Suddenly, it felt like the building was falling out from under me, leaving me suspended in the air. My stomach dropped, and the walls, chairs, ceiling, and floor all disappeared. I didn't hear music anymore. All I could hear was stillness. Not silence, but stillness, like when you're standing in a forest and just for a moment the wind stops and it feels like the entire world is holding its breath. Total stillness. Donita was nowhere to be found.

I looked around to try to get my bearings, and all I could see was light. I was in a place that seemed to be composed entirely of light, a light that could spin and swirl. It was translucent and it felt alive. I could feel the gentle warmth of the light on my face and hands. While I had never been to this place before, it felt familiar like an old childhood home feels familiar. The place in which I stood had no walls; it was only a ceiling and a floor that seemed to go on forever. And it was so bright that I could hardly open my eyes.

After a few seconds, I began to blink and squint, trying to see a little better. As I got used to the brightness, I could make out the silhouette of a figure walking toward me. I had no fear of the figure. I didn't know what was happening, but I knew somehow that everything would be okay.

As the silhouette grew, I saw the figure of a man approaching me. I saw the dark, leathery skin on his work-worn hands and face as he finally came into view. I saw his shaggy brown hair and the wide smile on his face. I saw his eyes. It seemed like somehow, all the radiance and otherworldly beauty of this room had been a cheap imitation of the reality hidden in his eyes. His eyes were *every* color—even colors I had never seen before. They were deep and intense and overflowing with love for me.

He held his hand out to me and said, in a deep, soft voice, like a big, thick blanket on a cold winter night, "Mattie, I am so glad you're here. Come with me. I've prepared a place for you!"

As his hand reached to take hold of mine, I looked down and saw that there was a hole through it. It was an image that jarred me enough that I then noticed the scars that ran from his hands, all the way up his arm, and onto his neck, and even his face and head. They were gruesome and ugly. They were the opposite of everything I'd ever imagined about meeting Jesus.

He took me by the hand, but I hesitated, still shocked by the ghastly scars that marred his skin. He stopped and turned back, and as I ran my thumb across the hole in his hand, I asked, "Did it hurt?"

He turned back to face me, his eyes welling with tears just a bit. He smiled a knowing smile that made his eyes curve over the top of his cheeks. Never letting go of my hand, seeming to want to draw my attention to the significance of the moment, he looked around the brilliant space we were in, then back at me. After some time, he took a deep breath and said softly, "It was worth it."

And just as suddenly as I had found myself in that place, I found myself back in Donita's church. Only now, I was lying on the ground in front of my seat, soaked in my own tears and shaking like a leaf. I laid there for what might have been hours trying to compose myself. Had I really just been with Jesus? How unbelievable that, when asked about the indescribable pain He endured on the cross, His response would be a simple, loving "It was worth it." What kind of love is this that would consider the suffering of Calvary a price worth paying to be with me? ...*ME!*

I felt very small that day. But I had stood face-to-face with a very big love. And while honestly, I am still processing what I experienced that day, I knew then—just as I know now—that this love is able to carry me through anything I could ever face.

Chapter 3

THAT TIME I MET SOME CHRISTIANS

Gandhi once famously said, "I like your Christ, but I do not like your Christians." For many years I agreed with him. I liked Jesus, but in my experience, there weren't really any Christians who looked much like him at all. I was convinced—as many other people are—that Christians were closed-minded, hypocritical snobs who thrived on exclusivity and self-advancement. I thought church was like a country club, where nice looking, well-off people came together to hide from the dirty world outside, and congratulate each other on their success and importance. All the while, I, and the rest of *For Today*, were out in the trenches, loving a forgotten subculture of people, and sharing Jesus with those the mainstream church didn't like to think about. *They could really learn a thing or two from us*, I would think to myself.

One night, as we continued on our great American rock-and-roll adventure, we came into Tulsa, Oklahoma. We'd been to Tulsa a few times before, and we had some friends there who were kind

enough to let us sleep on their floor when we were in the area. This

particular night, as we drove through their neighborhood, we

passed a massive parking lot that was packed full of cars. A big red

and white sign that towered over the cars and shone out into the

darkness read, "Rhema Bible Institute."

Our friends were students there. Privately I thought the idea

of spending years of your life *studying* ministry, instead of just

walking outside and *doing* ministry was insanity (as well as a

complete waste of money...), but I managed to bite my tongue

when the subject would come up. We asked our friends why the

parking lot was full so late at night, and they said something about

there being a formal banquet there that night.

About an hour later, after we'd gotten to the house and

carried our sleeping bags and backpacks inside, Mike and I had a

great idea: we should walk over to Rhema Bible Institute and crash

their alumni banquet. The worst-case scenario, we reasoned, was

we'd get kicked out and have to come back to the house. Best-case scenario...we'd get to eat some free food. The potential reward definitely outweighed the risk to us, so we set off.

I should explain one more thing. At that point in our lives, we weren't the inviting, insanely handsome young men we are now; we looked like homeless people. Mike's beard had gotten seriously radical at that point. I don't think he had shaved or cut his hair in the <u>year</u> since I joined the band, so he had a sandy blonde mane that hung down almost to his shoulders in a tangled frame to his face, and flowed straight into the sides of his long, wild, brown beard. I wore a dirty, military green trench coat that smelled like I'd pulled it out of a dumpster. It hung loosely over my plain white t-shirt that still carried the remnants of the sweaty concerts and sloppy meals we'd had over the last few weeks. I also had dread locks that hung down to my belly button and two lip rings.

It's completely safe to say we didn't look a thing like Bible school students.

We started the short trip over to the campus, imagining as we walked, how unwelcome poor, dirty people like us probably

43

must be in places like that. We prepared ourselves to be turned away by some well-dressed, smiley Republicans shortly after walking through the door. I was very confident that my opinions would be confirmed, and that that night I would find one more reason to add to my list of reasons why mainstream Christians were not to be trusted.

As we approached the door, I was a little nervous, but I didn't say anything—that wouldn't have been manly. Instead I took a deep breath and we walked through the door into a massive room about the size of a gymnasium, that was full of, just as we expected, nicely-dressed people sitting at round tables, eating what smelled like a great meal. At that point we realized that we hadn't planned for anything beyond walking in the door, so we just stood there awkwardly.

Right on cue, we noticed two men in button up shirts and ties walking our way. I braced myself for the unwelcome, "Um... Can we help you?" but it never came. The first man, who I believe was the boss, approached us with a smile and his hand stretched out to shake mine. He greeted me and looked me in the eye, and said, "Hi guys, my name's Jim! Have y'all had anything to eat yet?"

He introduced himself to Mike just as enthusiastically as he did me and continued, "We've got an awesome spread here. Let me grab y'all some seats and we'll get you a plate!"

We were just as confused as we probably looked. There was no time to think. We followed Jim through the crowd, weaving in between tables until he found a couple open seats on the far right side of the room. He sat us down, and pleasantly introduced "Mike and Mattie" to the rest of the table.

The other people there didn't seem intimidated by us at all, which...I have to admit, I was a little disappointed by. They asked where we were from and how we'd ended up at the banquet. After a couple minutes servers brought us our plates, and we ate and chatted with the others at our table, doing our best to not offend their courteous sensibilities with our sort of institutionalized, sloppy, band-guy demeanor.

At that point in our career, Taco Bell was a luxury. We didn't know how to handle the meal we'd been given or the company with whom we sat, but they kept the conversation going. They asked questions and seemed genuinely interested in who we were. We told them about our band and our heart for seeing people come to know Christ. They asked all about our songs and wanted to know how they could hear our music. With smiles on their faces, they celebrated and encouraged us, and they told us how important our ministry was and how thankful they were to have met us. They were—dare I say it—*kind*.

After a while, a well-dressed man made his way to the stage to welcome the crowd and share his heart for a bit. I didn't know who he was, though everyone else seemed to. He spent a lot more time talking about Jesus than he did talking about the school. I remember at one point I knew things were getting serious because he unbuttoned his suit jacket to be able to wave his arms more emphatically while he talked. After some time, with tears in his eyes, he passionately implored the audience to remember what was important—that they continue to live their lives to make Jesus famous. To represent Him well in all things. And to never give up.

As he finished, he invited those in attendance to join him in prayer. The people seated at our table didn't hesitate to reach out and take our hands. We bowed our heads, connected now to the heart we'd experienced in that place, and joined with them as they approached God.

He finished praying and dismissed the crowd, but many more people came over to meet us before we left. We definitely stood out from the crowd, but each of them, with enthusiasm, excitement, and love brought encouragement, advice, and support for not only our ministry, but us as well. The group of people at that Bible school embraced and celebrated us like no one ever had, and they confronted us with a reality that Gandhi had apparently never considered...

Some Christians actually look like Christ.

REVIVAL OF RELATIONSHIP

I know that this part of the book is probably kind of boring. I mean, the story basically goes, "I went to a Christian school, and they were nice to me." I get it. This scene probably won't make the movie adaptation of this book. But to say that this event changed my life would be an understatement, so I needed to include it.

You have to understand my perspective at this point in my life. I was convinced that all Christians were hypocritical elitists who shunned anyone different from themselves, and twisted the words of Christ to justify that behavior. I spoke openly about how destructive "organized religion" was, exhorting my followers to not get caught up in going to "church," because you could "be the church" wherever you wanted. While I considered myself a Christian, I would cringe every time the word was used to describe me, for fear that I'd be lumped in to the same category as some of these people I disdained so vehemently.

I didn't realize that Christ and His bride (the Church) are inseparably linked. If you try to be my friend, but you hate my wife, our friendship won't last very long at all. In the same way that you don't get a relationship with Mattie without developing one with Candice, you won't get a relationship with Jesus without developing one with His bride as well. After Jesus drew me in to encounter *Him*, the natural next step was for Him to draw me in to encounter *His people*!

If it weren't for the kind, radical, loving people I met at Rhema Bible Institute, I may never have preached in a church. I fear I might have cut myself off completely from any Christian fellowship outside of my band, likely succumbed to the pressures of the music industry, and fallen away from the faith altogether as we've seen many other Christian band members do. If it wasn't for the people I met that night who represented the heart of God to me so well, I might have stayed convinced that no one could teach me anything, and I would never have learned who I could really become in Him. What a beautiful moment of understanding God's grace and purpose.

In the years since that night, I've seen thousands upon thousands of people make decisions for Christ at conferences or church events at which I have ministered. And, if it wasn't for a few believers being unafraid to cross cultural boundaries to come meet, celebrate, and encourage Mike and I that night—confronting us with the reality of a Kingdom of people we didn't really believe could exist—none of that would ever have happened.

Never underestimate the power of connecting with other Christians. In fact, Jesus said, "The world will know you are my disciples by the way you love *one another*." (John 13:35) If we, as the Church, will not love each other, then our ambitions and even our best laid plans to reach the world will fail before they begin. It is by our love for *each other* that we prove to the world that the Gospel we carry is true, and powerful, and able to save. This is not a message we can tell them, they must see it for themselves.

Chapter 4

EXHALE LOVE

Love is a bit like air. Without it, we're doomed. But it's not enough to simply have it around us, we need to find a way to get it *inside* us. To simply believe that love exists will do us little good, as it is only by *receiving* it that it can ever sustain us. And receiving love might be the bravest, most challenging thing we will ever have to do.

That time I met Jesus was overwhelming, to say the least. It was like I'd been tossed into a violent flood of affection, swept up, and carried away into a new reality, a place where I could see my old life, but all my perceptions and priorities had changed. As profoundly transformative as that moment was, I was only just beginning to let this love inside me. As it began to seep into me, I saw it begin to reach out and touch others, as it reached out to me that memorable time I met some Christians.

The band continued pressing on, grinding our way through a never-ending list of tour dates. We played over 300 concerts in 2008. Some of them were amazing, many were not. But at each one we would share the love of God with anyone who cared to listen.

One night, I stood onstage in Seattle and shared the gospel with a room full of people as they lifted their middle fingers, screaming and spitting at me for it. Just a few months later, we were back to the same room in the same bar; I shared the same Gospel, and we saw prayer circles break out and hundreds of people encounter the love of Jesus.

I would preach the Gospel from the stage to whatever crowd was there, regardless of how receptive they were. And when we weren't on stage, we would strike up conversations about life, faith, and love with people in gas stations, grocery stores, or malls — wherever we happened to be.

The band's popularity was growing quickly at that point, though the support we got from within the music industry was more or less non-existent. I remember hearing that a number of well-known record labels (even one very influential *Christian* record label), many booking agents, and other music industry types, were hesitant to work with us. They were *sure* that a band as outspoken and overt about their faith as we were could never really achieve much success.

We didn't care. We just kept going.

Eventually, the beautiful people at Facedown Records decided to roll the dice with us, signing us to a 3-album deal, and actually celebrating our boldness for the Gospel. I don't know if they were very kind or very crazy, but we were grateful for them.

We made friends in cities all around the nation who were kind enough to share our music with those in their circle, and as word spread about who we were and what we stood for, the crowds began to grow. Some people were excited about our music, some were excited about our ministry. We weren't too picky—we were just happy that people were coming to be a part of the adventure God had sent us on.

STRANGERS' FLOORS

Candice and I continued to grow closer, despite the distance and the insanity of my schedule. One day, at a mall in Zanesville, Ohio, I spent every last cent I had to buy her an engagement ring. It cost $330. I couldn't afford to eat for a few days after that, but I was happy with the decision. I managed to keep it a secret and finally proposed to her a couple months later.

We started excitedly planning our transition into marriage, and as the date crept closer, we made and then broke plans to get an apartment in Alabama. Miraculously, Candice wanted to come on tour with me and the rest of the band. I was, obviously, *very* excited, but I was pretty sure she didn't know what she was in for. This beautiful, delicate flower of a girl was about to quit her job as a banker, leave her childhood home, and move into a van with her new husband and his five best friends.

Now, I think I should explain to you what tour was like at this point in our career. We couldn't afford a tour bus. We had a van—one of those white, 15-passenger, "free candy" vans. We couldn't afford hotels, so we spent half our nights in the van, driving to wherever our next show was scheduled (a monotonous thing, only broken up by the occasional late night truck stop adventure). The other half of our nights were spent on the living room floor of anyone generous (or reckless) enough to invite a metal band into their home for the night.

That was the reality my new wife was about to step into. Our wedding day arrived—January 24, 2009—and it was beautiful! She was the most indescribably stunning thing I've ever seen. And then, less than two weeks later, we all piled back into the van, this time with one more body in the group. With no fanfare and our eyes set on the horizon, we hit the trail again. My new wife and I— piled up awkwardly on a little bench in our van, or sleeping uncomfortably on a stranger's floor—were maybe too naïve to know, or too excited to care, that this wasn't what marriage was supposed to look like. We had no desire to fit the mold.

I slept countless nights sitting up with my face pressed against the cold glass of the vibrating van window, holding my beautiful wife's legs sprawled out across my lap. Showers were often hard to come by and we ate almost exclusively fast food. Even during the short breaks from being on tour, we had no home to go back to. We had an air mattress in Iowa or a futon in Ohio that were available to us as needed, but, for the first two years of our marriage, that little gray bench in the back of our big white van was the closest thing we had to a home.

This life we volunteered for was anything but glamorous, but we were together and we were utterly convinced that what we were doing was *important*. That made it all worthwhile.

THE HARDEST LESSON I EVER LEARNED

Just a few days into Candice's first tour with us, we had a concert in Waco, Texas. It was a great night – the show was well attended and we met a lot of new friends. After we performed, Candice and I stood outside the venue as we did most nights, chatting with show-goers and praying for people.

Toward the end of the night, a group of three young people came up to talk with us. There was a boy named Matt and his

56

girlfriend, Aubrey. Matt had tan skin and long, stringy, almond-colored hair. He looked like one of the Lost Boys from Neverland. Aubrey was a sweet, bubbly girl with bright blue eyes and a big, infectious smile. She had a round face that was framed by her straight, blonde hair, and kept her fingers tightly wrapped up with Matt's.

Matt and Aubrey both came up and greeted us enthusiastically, but their friend, Sam, stood a few feet behind them. Sam was much taller than Matt and seemed mostly uninterested in the situation, though he stuck around to hear what I might have to say. His hands were in his pockets and his eyes wandered around the parking lot, taking in the wildly colorful, bustling crowd all huddled together in little groups in the darkness outside the venue. All three of them smelled a bit like alcohol.

As we did every night, Candice and I asked our new friends what, if anything, they knew about God, then we listened. Some people will say very beautiful things if you give them the chance. All of them had a bit to say on the subject – they lived in Texas, after all – and Candice shared a bit of her story with them.

"I used to have a serious drinking problem," she said, capturing Aubrey's attention right away. "I remember when I was in college, coming to concerts like this, and getting drunk in the parking lot before I went in."

Aubrey and Matt listened intently.

"But I found Jesus...or maybe He found me. And He loved me like no one in the world ever could."

At this, Aubrey opened up a bit about how difficult things had been for her over the last few years; about the abuse she had suffered and the failures of her parents.

Candice persisted gently, "I just want you to know that God loves you. I mean, He *really* loves you. He's a father to the fatherless and His perfect love never fails!"

We continued sharing our hearts with the group, and as it seemed to begin to sink in for them, I asked if they wanted to pray with us. They lived in Waco and we lived in a van, so we didn't know if or when we'd ever see them again. Ultimately, we told them, what they *really* needed was *Jesus*, not us—and if they would simply ask Him, He would make Himself very real to each of them.

Matt was the first to volunteer for prayer. He asked if we could pray for him to find friends that could help teach him about Jesus. We prayed, and then we hugged, and it felt like family. Aubrey was excited at the opportunity to pray as well. Candice laid her hand on Aubrey's shoulder and sweetly offered up simple adoration to God. She asked that He would help Aubrey know Him as a father, and that His love would invade her life like we'd seen it do for so many others before her. Aubrey cried onto Candice's shoulder. Something really beautiful happened there in the parking lot on that cool, still Texas night. Strangers became friends, and scared kids found real peace in an unlikely place.

As Aubrey regained her composure, she turned to Sam and waved him forward. Matt followed suit, turning and asking Sam, "Do you want to pray too?"

I said to Sam, "Man, God really loves you. You don't have to have this all figured out. It's okay to have questions. If you want, you can just ask God to *show* you if He really is out there."

There was a hesitation, a few precious seconds where Sam considered. Then his cold demeanor returned, and he replied sternly, "No, man. I'm my own god."

"Okay," I replied quickly. "I'm not mad at you, man. Just want you to know that we really *do* love you."

"Okay," he said, looking away again and stuffing his hands back into his pockets.

With that, we hugged our new friends goodbye and sent them off with words of encouragement and advice. We thanked them for their time, and reminded Matt and Aubrey that things were about to change for them. They had just spoken with a *real* God, who is *really* alive, and who *really* hears their prayers. We waved as they disappeared into the darkness of the night, and we walked back inside.

Two days later, I got a phone call from a number I didn't recognize. I answered, and the voice on the other end said, "Hi, is this Mattie?"

"Yes…"

"Hi. Uh… This is Gabe. I was in charge of booking for your show in Waco just the other day."

"Oh, hi Gabe!" I said.

"The reason I'm calling is… Do you remember talking with some kids at the show named Aubrey and Matt?" He had an uncomfortable quiver in his voice.

"Yes."

"Well…there was an accident."

My mind was racing. "Oh no…!"

"On the way home from your concert, they were riding with their friend Sam. Sam was going too fast around a curve and his car flipped. Aubrey and Matt are in the hospital, but they'll both be

61

okay. Aubrey just woke up, and the first thing she said to her nurse is that she needed to talk with Candice."

"Okay. We can definitely do that." I replied. "But what about Sam?"

Gabe paused for a minute, needing to regain his composure. "Sam died, Mattie. He was killed in the accident."

"Okay," I murmured with tears in my eyes, clearing my throat and trying to breathe. "Thank you for letting us know. I'll have Candice get in touch with Aubrey as soon as possible."

"Thank you," he replied as I hung up the phone. I wept.

As I relayed the message to Candice, the weight of what had happened began to bear down upon her as well. Our friend Sam— the one who had rejected prayer, saying, "I'm my own god," had died only *minutes* after those words left his lips. Sam would never get the chance to reconsider his statements. He would never have the opportunity to do his own research and come to his own conclusions about God. Sam would never again attend a church service, or hear a Gospel presentation. Our friend Sam had died. We were the last people to have really spoken with him, and the last conversation he had on earth ended with an invitation for him to come to Christ. An invitation he declined.

When I told Sam I loved him that night, I really meant it. None of us knew that that would be his last night on earth. But even in Sam's final hour, God, with incredible love, was *still* calling him. Still holding the door of grace open just a little while longer.

Sometimes I get tired of ministry. Sometimes I don't like awkward conversations. Sometimes it's messy and uncomfortable and time-consuming to have to walk with people through their fears and doubts. Sometimes I think maybe I should just mind my own business. *It'll be fine if I don't say anything this time*, I tell myself. But then I remember the night I met Sam. I remember the devastating hours and days my wife and I spent weeping for him and his family after we heard the news of his death. I remember how heart-broken his friends were. I also remember that *sometimes*, for *some* people, *there won't be a tomorrow.*

Remembering that gives me the strength and patience to forget myself and choose to love them today.

Sam's death deepened my conviction to make love *my* responsibility, right here and right now. I would not dismiss the common moments in life or the people who occupy them with me—like the girl handing me a coffee at the Starbucks drive-through window, or the guy ringing me up in the checkout line at a grocery store. I would choose to really *engage* people, to *see* them, and to *love* them where they're at. I stopped waiting for "big" moments to share this big love, and I began to share it freely. And as I did so, I learned that big love can make a small moment a big deal.

Chapter 5

WHAT I LEARNED IN JAPAN

In March of 2011, a massive tsunami devastated the coast of Japan, killing over 16,000 people. Three days later, we landed there for the first day of our tour. To say that was awkward timing would be an understatement.

First of all, our band was not very popular in Japan. Second of all, their nation had just suffered the most significant natural disaster in its history—I don't think anyone in Japan was really too interested in stage diving right then. But, we were there, determined to do our best, see the sights, and share Jesus with people.

Japan is a really wonderful place. It's clean and bright and full of beautiful olive-skinned people. I saw one other black guy while we were there (it was easy to spot each other because we were both about one foot taller than everyone else in the country); we nodded in respectful recognition of each other and continued on our way. People in Japan are kind, and quiet, and considerate. It's pretty much the opposite of the United States.

The most significant difference, I think, was that, in Japan, *nobody* spoke *any* English. We had done some overseas touring prior to this, and all throughout Europe, people were at least a *little* familiar with English. The same was true in Central and South America—they may not have been fluent, but they could say "hello" and maybe help you find the bathroom or the library or whatever other general location you, as a foreigner, may be desperately in need of. That was definitely *not* the case in Japan. When I asked someone a question in English, they would stare at me blankly, like I'd walked up to them and meowed like a cat.

We had a tour manager named Toru. He had organized our trip, and he was in charge of driving us around Japan during the week we were scheduled to be there. Even *he* didn't speak any English. He was with us all day every day, and he never really said much. Sometimes he would speak Japanese very slowly, as if that would somehow be easier for people who don't speak any Japanese to understand. If he absolutely *had* to communicate something to us, he would type it into a translator app he had on his phone that never really worked right. It was every bit as awkward as you're probably imagining.

We arrived for the first concert, excited and honored to be in Japan, but a little uncertain about how it would go. I stood on stage in front of the crowd that had come, and as I had done hundreds of times before, I preached the Gospel with zeal and vigor, inviting the crowd to behold the mighty love of Jesus that was for them in that place. And they—like everyone else I'd talked to in Japan—stared at me blankly, like I'd walked up on stage and meowed like a cat. Nobody understood a word I said. Eventually, we got the message, and just went on to the next song, but my mind was racing. What was I going to do? Why was I even t*here* if I couldn't communicate with these people? It was as strange a scenario as I'd ever been in.

PRAYING THROUGH

Eventually I came to terms with the fact that no matter how badly I wanted to be the guy that shared Jesus with these people, I simply couldn't be. No matter how much I wanted to be the one to tell them all about what He had done for me, and what He could do for them, I couldn't speak their language, and they couldn't speak mine. I couldn't stand in the spotlight of ministry before this group of people. I was stuck; burdened for the people of Japan, but not able to be involved in what God was doing there. It was discouraging. Honestly, it felt a bit like we were wasting our time, playing music for people we couldn't talk to, in a nation that had much more pressing issues at that time than buying a t-shirt from some metal band from the United States.

One night, though, we played a concert in a city called Osaka. After the show, Toru drove us to our hotel for the evening. As we unloaded our bags and walked inside, I looked across the street and saw a big red cross on the outside of a building, with a giant sign, written in English: OSAKA EVANGELISTIC TABERNACLE. I

68

was happy to think that, even if *I* was not able to share Jesus with the people of Japan, *someone* could. So I thought, "I should pray for them."

I handed my backpack to Ryan, our guitarist, and said, "I'll meet you up in the room in a few minutes." With that, I left the rest of the group, and headed out across the dark street and onto the sidewalk in front of this church. It was maybe 1 a.m. at this point and no one was around. I didn't mind; I wasn't there to meet people or get a tour of the facility, I was there to pray into what God was doing in the nation of Japan.

I stood bathed in the golden-orange glow of the streetlights that hung, humming unassumingly over the sidewalk in front of the church. It was a big, tan building, covered with signs painted in bold, red letters—most of them Japanese. Crosses decorated every sign and structure of the building, leaving no doubt what this place represented. There was a concrete wall around the church, and a metal gate that was tightly chained shut and locked. Toward the top of the concrete wall, running all along the sidewalk, were television sets, maybe six of them in total. Each of the televisions played the same thing: A video of evangelist Reinhard Bonnke preaching the Gospel at Hillsong Church in Australia, with Japanese subtitles.

There was no fanfare or ceremony; I just began to pray. It was nothing spectacular at first, I started praying for the pastors and the leaders at the church. I prayed that God would maintain their integrity and conviction, that they would have clear vision and be strengthened to continue running the race He had set before them.

Continuing to pray, going deeper and lifting up the marriages and families in the church, I felt the presence of God begin to surround and overwhelm me, like a rushing wind that swept down that dark Osaka street straight into the deep places of my heart. I began to weep and shake and pray with greater fervor than ever before. When I prayed for those who would come to Christ through the ministry of that church, visions of multitudes began springing up in my mind's eye. I saw the streets in front of the church closed because thousands upon thousands of people, in

70

their desperation to encounter the living God, were flocking to this place. I saw many healed, delivered, and made free and alive by the great love that the Father wanted to display through that place, and I began to call these things into existence – to celebrate the things that had not happened yet, and thank God for His faithfulness to send people to proclaim His Kingdom in this place that I had come to love so much in such a short amount of time.

I was caught up now. "Five or ten minutes" turned quickly into an hour, then an hour and a half. I started to lose my voice, but kept on—dripping sweat and praying frantically and feverishly for these beautiful people, my brothers and sisters in faith that I knew I would likely never meet. I was utterly convinced that God had wonderful and glorious intentions for them, and that night, as I invested my time, sweat, and tears into seeing those intentions become a reality, I was able to join with these people in the work of the ministry for Japan. I would never be the man in the spotlight, but I was honored to simply be the one in the dark, on the sidewalk, lifting up the man—whoever he would be—to the place God would bring him to love and serve that nation well.

THE LITTLE LADY

Suddenly, out of the deep darkness of what had become early morning, I saw a figure break into my special moment with the God of the universe. It was a woman. A little Japanese woman, walking lightly up the sidewalk with her round face and messy hair. She was wearing a baggy black sweatshirt that wasn't quite large enough to cover her round, pregnant belly. As she came closer to me, I think she noticed that something was happening, although I'm sure it looked more like insanity than glory to her. She stopped maybe 30 feet away from me, and after curiously watching me pray and worship for a brief moment, she turned to face one of the TV screens.

We both stayed there for a while—me hysterically praying for people I couldn't even talk to, and her quietly taking in the strange words on a Japanese TV screen being preached by a

72

German evangelist to Africa during an event at an Australian church.

After what must have been ten minutes, with my eyes closed and salty tears still staining my cheeks, I felt a tug on my sleeve. The woman had broken herself away from the TV and come over to get my attention.

She started speaking to me in slow, uncertain Japanese, and the smell of alcohol wafted up from her tiny frame. This little, pregnant Japanese woman was drunk—very drunk. When she finally paused, overwhelmed with compassion for her and disappointment at the situation, I said, "I'm so sorry. I don't speak Japanese."

She looked at me blankly for a brief moment, and then she squinted her eyes like she had an idea. Then, this little, drunk, pregnant Japanese woman turned and pointed at the TV screen, looked up at me, and said in *perfect* English, "First time. Teach me."

I was dumbfounded. This was the most English anyone had spoken to me the whole time I'd been here. I certainly didn't expect it in this setting, on a dark street, outside a random church, at 3 o'clock in the morning. But there we were – the crazy, praying American boy, and the drunk, pregnant Japanese lady – living in that moment together.

I searched my mind and heart, anxiously trying to find a way to relay to her the more important parts of the message. I started and stopped a few times, realizing seconds into my spiel that she wasn't following. The message had to get simpler. I remembered something I once read in the Bible: Philippians 2 says, "God has highly exalted Him, and given Him the name that is above *every* name, so that at the name of Jesus, every knee should bow, in heaven and on earth and under the earth, and every tongue confess that Jesus Christ is Lord, to the glory of God the Father."

What was my message for this woman? It was Jesus! That's it. Easy. Simple. Jesus. I said the name, "Jesus," to her, motioning for her to repeat after me. I believed that somehow, there was power in the name to revolutionize her life—to make her free from the alcohol habit that could harm her baby, and to give her instead such a hunger for Him that she might come back to this church during the day, and find people that could teach her who Jesus really is and what He has really done.

"J—Jesus?" she whispered.

I smiled.

"Jesus!" she proclaimed again, much more confidently. Her face changed. The weight of her drunkenness seemed to lift off of her right in front of me, and a light began to shine in her eyes. She smiled a wide, innocent smile, and then she wrapped her arms around my waist. I held this little Japanese woman in my arms, and I prayed for her in English. I asked God to make her the first of *many* people that would meet Him there at Osaka Evangelistic Tabernacle. I asked God to make her free, and to fill her with joy, to show her *His* purpose for her life, and to sweep her up with His love. She didn't understand a word I said. But there, under an orange street light, in the middle of the night, on a dark Japanese street, two people from different worlds came together with nothing to stand on but that beautiful name. *Jesus.*

I will never forget that night on the street in Osaka. I have never felt less adequate or less qualified for ministry. But I learned that for every need, God has an answer, and sometimes, that answer is not me. I will probably never be the voice of a mighty awakening in Japan, and that's okay. Maybe that little Japanese lady might! And, no matter what, I know God loves those people, and he has someone there who *can* share the good news of Jesus with them! Japan will be saved.

During our time on tour in Japan, I learned the hard lesson that it was time to take myself out of the spotlight and put Jesus back into it.

My job was never to reach the world—that's *His* job. My job is to do what I can, where I can, how I can, and to leave the rest up to Him.

Chapter 6

IN MY SHOES

As time went on, the crowds grew and the shows got bigger. At first it was a subtle trickle of new followers, but then, seemingly overnight, the small groups of people who once came to our shows turned into a sea of faces. Suddenly, we weren't just kids playing basements and local bars anymore, we were a real band, playing real concerts.

There is nothing in the world quite like performing at one of our shows. Each night, I stand in the room and just breathe, closing my eyes and making a genuine effort to truly *be* there in that moment. The air is thick with the stench of sweat, stale beer being sold from the tap behind the bar and spilled on the floor by people who ordered one too many, and cigarettes being smoked in the secret shadows of the night. As we stand backstage, we can hear the faint sound of the crowd murmuring and moving about on the floor, waiting for the moment we go on. No one knows when it's coming, but no one can miss it when it arrives. Eventually, after what seems like an eternity, the background music fades and every light in the room dims. It starts with a brief stillness, followed by a low rumble of excitement across the room, then the sound builds until the crowd is roaring in anticipation. The five of us make our way onto the stage and it feels like time stands still. We all sort of hold our breath—each member sensing the timing and intention of the others. Then all together, just as we've rehearsed countless times, the instruments, the voices, the lights, and the fans explode into a wild, chaotic orchestra that is, I think, much more strongly felt than it is seen or heard.

Surprisingly, in the frenzy, there is some order to be found. Those who know the words best press their way through the hoard to make sure I can see them as they sing. Sometimes, as I scan the crowd, I lock eyes or hold hands with a singing fan, connecting with them in a brief serendipitous moment. In the middle of the tempest around us, we acknowledge each other's soul, and it becomes easy to forget that there is anyone else in the room.

Behind the muddled mob of a choir pressed up toward the front of the room are the moshers. They may know the words, but they're more interested in being moved. Maybe it's the way they're wired, but they just can't stand still once the music starts. They pace back and forth like wild beasts, waiting to find their moment of utter, unrelenting, violent freedom. Sometimes they punch people in the face. It's not on purpose though—that's just kind of how it goes. Don't stand near the mosh pit if you can't handle getting punched. Or kicked. Or slammed into.

Behind the pit, you have the spectators. Spectators are people who may or may not know our band or be familiar with our songs. They're those who, for various reasons, have decided they want to *watch* the concert as opposed to being steamrolled by it. That's where parents and casual fans hang out, as well as the people who pretty much go to concerts to show off their cool new outfit. They're there, but they're standing at a safe distance.

As the music carries us along and the massive, pounding speakers drive the music into us, the lights spin and flicker along.

Here and there fans find their way up on top of the sea of bodies, and they crowd surf toward me. We grab hands as they make it to the front of the crowd and we sing together for a few seconds. Then they're gone, just as suddenly as they appeared—back into the indiscernible chaos of the night, to find their friends and share their story.

Somewhere in the midst of it all, the hundreds or thousands in the room seem to become one. Many different people standing as one crowd. Many different voices singing one song.

For me, the most magical thing about performing is seeing those people—all of whom arrived that night with their own set of political or religious ideologies, their own secrets and their own fears—as they are finally able to lay down the messiness of their private lives. They've come together, and found a place where they can stand with strangers on common ground, and celebrate a common passion. There, in dark music venues, in those hot, summer nights, strangers become family. It's the way life is supposed to be.

Those beautiful moments of unity and expression, as all good things do, eventually come to an end. So with our fists in the air and our ears ringing, the guitars scream one last time and we bow in acknowledgement of the fans. We are grateful to them and for them. Our time is over, and we walk out of the spotlight. The magic of these moments is not found in the music or the lights, but in the passion of people—all the same in our uniqueness—coming together to burn for something greater than themselves. That is where the magic lives.

Just as suddenly as it began, the show ends and the moment begins to fade. The thick, intoxicating atmosphere of wild freedom and awe is relegated to a collection of stories or photos. We can never recapture the magic and raw power of those moments, but we keep our photos as a window through which we can look back, and remember what it felt like to stand as one with so many others. We were a part of something bigger than ourselves, and it felt like we might change the world.

COMING DOWN

When I walk off stage, with my ears ringing and sweat burning my bloodshot eyes, for a moment I just breathe. Those moments on stage are a high that is sometimes hard to come down from. The other members of the band and crew go about the busy process of unplugging and repacking a million cables, instruments, and tools, but there is none of that for me—only my ringing ears belying the deafening stillness that stands in stark contrast to the roaring chaos of moments prior.

After I collect myself, dry my face, and change out of my sweat-soaked t-shirt, I take a deep breath and make my way outside. That's where the fans are—and they are the inspiration and reason for this whole thing, after all. I go out to meet anyone who happens to be hanging around.

Walking through the crowd of people after one of our shows is a bit like a scene from a zombie movie. Every zombie movie has it, you know the one...where the main characters have to try to quietly sneak through a crowd of unsuspecting zombies? Inevitably, someone kicks a soda can, and one of the zombies looks and goes, "Blaarrrgh," then all the other zombies turn to see what's happening, and the hero and his cute girlfriend have to run away to keep from getting eaten. It's not *exactly* like that, but a little bit.

Every time, someone yells, "Hey Mattie! Can I get a quick picture?" Then they ask their friend to take it for them and hand him their camera. He takes a quick 15 minutes to figure out how the camera works, while we smile and pose and make awkward small talk. Then their friend who took the picture wants a picture of his own, so they swap places. I smile and pose again. Then, other people start to wonder what all the picture taking is about. They see "the guy from For Today" standing there, and they murmur a bit and gather in closer, alerting their friends to the excitement. Then one thing leads to another, and the next thing you know, the fans are eating my intestines.

The people wait their turn (usually), and one by one, we smile politely and make small talk. I thank them for coming, and try to graciously receive any compliments they may have for our music or our performance. I answer questions like, "So, how's tour been?" or "When are you coming back to our city?" with stunning proficiency—just elaborate enough to satisfy the curiosity of the person who asked, but still expedient enough to be courteous to all the other people who are still waiting. I could have that conversation in my sleep. Sometimes I set my mental autopilot and stand through an hour of polite conversation, pulling out rehearsed answers to predictable questions, while privately trying to decide what kind of pizza I want to get after it's all over. I'm not really proud of that. No one seems to mind though.

I think it's often the low hum of monotony in our lives that can lull us into sleeping through what could have been our greatest moments. So I do my best to resist setting myself on auto-pilot and disengaging from these conversations. Even the predictable, seemingly insignificant moments can become something incredible if I'm willing to press a little further, willing to break the script and touch the hearts of the people with whom I speak. It may be a perfectly unremarkable conversation in a perfectly unremarkable moment, but the significance of a moment is not determined by the moment itself, but by the people who share it. After all, it's not a great moment that makes a man significant, it's a great man that makes a moment significant.

Author David Foster Wallace once wrote, "The more people think you're really great, the bigger the fear of being a fraud is." If I'm honest, I know that fear well. I stand there, smiling and shaking hands cordially; posing for pictures and signing autographs for those who have gathered, until everyone is satisfied. But there is a profound loneliness that finds me sometimes as I stand in a crowd of people who can love what I do, and ignore who I am.

I look around as strangers eagerly fiddle with their cameras and inch closer as their turn to talk with me approaches, and I wonder what all the fuss is about. I'm an ordinary man. And I wonder how very disappointed they might be with me if they ever got close enough to see just how ordinary I really am. But then I think, maybe it's nicer that people care at all—even if they care more about who they *think* I am, than who I *really* am.

The crowd dwindles after some time. The people have gotten what they came for. I give the last few hugs, handshakes, and hellos; I thank them for coming and wave as they head back to their houses. By that time, it's well after midnight, and I'm thankful the day is over. I shuffle back to my little spot in our van, and share stories of the night with the rest of the guys. We laugh about the awkward conversations we had, marvel at the amazing things God did in people's lives, and each help piece together the story of another wild night doing what we love, with people we love.

Eventually, that conversation, just like the others, begins to fade away like the last glowing embers of a fire and one by one, we slip off to sleep, knowing that we get to do it all over again tomorrow.

Chapter 7

MAX THE HOOLIGAN

One of the first times we toured Europe, I met Max. Max was a pizza guy and a rabid soccer fan from Liverpool, England. He showed me videos on his phone of some of his favorite goals from the last season, although I think that was mostly because he couldn't think of anything else to talk with me about. He was a fan of the band who came to see us play a concert in Liverpool and tracked me down out in the lobby after the show. He was a short guy with sandy blonde hair, combed off to the side like the type of boy a mom could be proud of, and he had a baby face—though he would probably be mad at me for writing that about him.

Eventually, Max ran out of soccer-related pleasantries, and said something that kind of shocked me. "I've never met a Christian before," he admitted. He wasn't trying to be disrespectful or accusatory at all, he was just genuinely admitting his unfamiliarity with the issue.

"Really?" I asked. (I live in Alabama. The idea of someone having never even *met* a Christian is absurd to me.)

"Yeah bro," he continued in his thick urban British accent. "I mean, I know about Christians—like, I know they're out there. I just never met one."

"That's awesome, man!" I said, excited to not have to try to undo 1,500 years of religious institutionalization for him.

Without any more coaxing, he offered up his thoughts on the subject. "Seems like a bunch of fairy tales if you ask me."

I hadn't asked him, but I was glad to have a starting point. "Why do you say that?" I asked.

"Well, you know. There's just no proof of any of it. I'm just supposed to believe it because it says so in some book?" He asked rhetorically.

I thought I'd test the waters, so I said, "Max, if you would take a look with me, I think I could show you that there's *plenty* of proof!"

I've never been the type to want to argue with people. If their mind is made up about wanting to live their life apart from God, I certainly can't change it for them. But, if they're interested in really searching it out—no matter how doubtful they may be—I'll help answer their questions however I can. That was the case with Max.

"I would love to believe if you think you can help me, bro," he said.

I motioned for him to follow me, and went for it. We walked down a side hallway to avoid being interrupted, and I starting telling Max stories. I told him about that time I met Jesus. I told him about how I'd met Candice, and how I'd been strangely handed money to go join the band. I shared with him every example I could think of, of God's actual, visible involvement in my life. And I *showed* him that in life, if you seek God, you *will* find him. Max listened intently, asking a lot of questions, and growing more excited as the conversation went on.

"You don't seem as crazy as I expected," he said at one point. He meant it as a compliment, so I took it as one. "I never thought about it like this before."

"Well, man, that's why I believe the way I do. I see God all around me all the time," I replied. "And you can too if you want. Max, we could pray together right now and ask God to be the God of your life, and to make Himself real to you."

"Oh, no thanks bro," he said immediately. "I mean, it's cool to get to hear all this from you, and it's nice to get to learn about God from you, but I don't think that is really for me."

"Okay, man," I said, moving on to another subject. Probably back to soccer.

Eventually, Max and I parted ways with a photo and a handshake, and he promised to come see us the next time we were in Liverpool.

THE ATHEIST PREACHER

Two days later, something strange happened. I was on stage in Manchester, and halfway through our set, I saw a familiar face run by me. It was Max! With a big smile on his face, he ran in front of me and dove off the stage into the crowd, turning to stick his tongue out and give me a thumbs up as he crowd-surfed out into the middle of the room. A little confused, but excited to see my new friend again, I moved on and finished the concert.

After our set was over, I went out into the crowd to meet people and take photos or sign autographs. After a few minutes, Max appeared again, standing at the back of the group waiting patiently for me to finish. After a minute or two, I think he got tired of waiting and he burst through the front of the line with his friend, Ben. Max introduced us to each other, and without stopping to take a breath, he launched into his wild story.

"Bro, after we talked, I kept thinking about all the stuff you said to me about God and Jesus. I didn't really believe it but it was so cool I couldn't stop thinking about it. So I was at work last night—I work at a pizza place with Benny here—and I started telling my friends what you told me...about meeting Jesus, and finding that ring on the ground and everything. They couldn't believe it either and Benny here wanted to come see you for himself. So we called in sick to work today and borrowed my mum's car to drive out to Manchester and see you again!"

As I stood there, just as confused as I was excited about everything he'd said, he continued. "I thought maybe you could teach us some more about Jesus."

I laughed in delight, amazed at Max's boldness. This boy, who didn't even believe in God, had walked into his work place and testified freely about the things God had done—even going so far as to invite his coworkers to come see for themselves!

I shared my story again with the two of them, answering some of the questions Ben had about the reliability of scripture and the "scary" God he'd heard was depicted in the Old Testament. As I spoke, some other people came up for a photo or an autograph, and Max would turn and welcome them into the conversation.

"He's talking about Jesus," he would inform them. "It's awesome. Come listen!"

So I went on. I shared about the miracles of Jesus and his death on the cross. I shared about sin and our need for a savior, and the hope that we have in Christ. I reminded them that, in the entire expanse of human history, there is and has only ever been *one* answer for the issue of sin, and that is the blood of Christ.

At the end of my hour-long recounting of all God had done for me, a group of about a dozen strangers had gathered. Ben and Max were even more excited than they were at the beginning of it all. Ben looked at Max with his mouth still open in amazement and said with all the beautiful innocence in the world, "I want to know Jesus."

Max nodded his head knowingly at his friend and turned to me saying, "Me too, bro."

With a big smile on my face I celebrated the boys' decision, I put one hand on each boy's shoulder and prayed that God would meet them where they were, and show them who He really is. I was even able to introduce them to a pastor friend of mine who lived in their area, so they could get around others who knew Jesus as well.

As I remember Max and his innocent enthusiasm about the things of God, I am inspired. He didn't know any Bible verses. He had never heard a sermon or attended a church service. Max didn't even *believe* in God, but he was genuine and authentic enough to walk into his workplace and share freely what he'd experienced— an act that gave his friend and many other strangers the opportunity to hear about the goodness of God and even to meet Him for themselves.

I liked Max. I kind of wanted to be more like Max. It's easy for me to forget that, while knowledge is a good thing, it's not a prerequisite to being a part of God's plan. Just like I learned in Japan, Max reminded me that it is not my ability to preach or recite Bible verses that qualifies me for the work of ministry, but rather an honest willingness to simply share what I personally have seen of God. It may not be much—in Max's situation, he wasn't even quite convinced of it himself—but if we are willing to share what we

have, we'll be surprised at the incredible things God is able to do
with it!

HANNAH'S ESCAPE

After we got back from our trip overseas, we took some

time off to rest. Candice and I still didn't have a place of our own, so

we visited her parents' house in Alabama. At one point during the

visit, I sat at their dining room table, answering e-mails, and found

that I had gotten a message from a woman who had reached out to

me in absolute desperation.

> *Mattie,*
>
> *I'm not sure if you'll ever actually read this, but I just felt like I needed to write you. It's about my daughter. Her name is Hannah. A few months ago, she cut off communication with me, and with everyone else associated with our church back home. She's moved in with her boyfriend, who is a Satanist, and she's developed a severe addiction to heroine. I know that recently, she was at a party, and she was gang-raped by a group of men. She got pregnant that night, and when her boyfriend found out, he took her to a clinic to get an abortion. I'm afraid for my daughter's safety and my heart is broken for her.*
>
> *The reason I'm writing you is because, I was on her Facebook page, and I noticed that she follows you. You are the only Christian influence in Hannah's*

*life right now, and I wondered if maybe you could
reach out to her and encourage her to come back to
Christ.*

Thank you. I am praying for you.

Shauna

Now, I have gotten messages from concerned parents

before, but something about this message particularly moved my

heart. I sat there at the dining room table with tears streaming

down my face, my heart burdened for this broken girl and her

worried family. I sat there and began to pray that God would

intervene in her life mightily, and that his love would break the

chains of addiction and bondage off of her life.

Often, when I get prayer requests sent to me, I'll pray for

them once and then move on. This one stayed with me, though.

The next day, I was still shaken by what I'd read; and the day after

that as well. After a few days of praying for this girl, I thought,

maybe I would reach out to her, and just let her know that God

loves her and still has a plan for her life.

I went to the Facebook page her mother had mentioned,

expecting to connect with Hannah through it. When I found the

96

page, though, I saw something I never could have expected. This "Satanist" boyfriend of hers was Marcus. I knew Marcus. In fact, he was the vocalist of a band I had gone on tour with once. Marcus wasn't a Satanist, he was an angry atheist who liked to *pretend* he was a Satanist to scare Christians. (There are a lot more people like that than you would think...) Marcus didn't scare me, and he really didn't like me either.

A bit caught off guard by the coincidence, it slowly dawned on me—I couldn't reach out to this girl at all. If Marcus knew that I was messaging his girlfriend behind his back, he'd have more than "I don't like you because you're a Christian" to hold against me. So, I didn't reach out to her at all. Instead, I did something really radical—I continued to pray.

I prayed every day. I was moved to tears for her often. Sometimes I prayed until my voice went hoarse. I cried out to God for her like she was my own daughter. In fact, at one point during this time, I was at a conference, and the preacher invited parents to come forward for prayer if they had children that needed to be saved. I *ran* to the altar even though I didn't have any kids at all; I was standing in Shauna's place—burdened for her beautiful daughter that had been so marred by the ugliness of the world.

After a few weeks of this, back on the road with the band again, a friend of mine came to a show, and asked me out of the blue if I had seen Marcus recently.

A little caught off guard, I said, "Uh...no man. Why do you ask?"

"I saw him the other day, and he told me that he wanted to track you down and *fight* you." My friend said, reveling in the scandal he had just welcomed me into.

"What?"

I hadn't told anyone but my wife that I'd been praying for Hannah. I racked my brain trying to figure out about how Marcus possibly could have known I was praying for her. I hadn't talked to her at all. I hadn't even told her mom that I was praying.

My friend continued, telling me a story that still seems as unbelievable today as it did when he first said it.

"Yeah man," he leaned in. "Marcus told me that last week, while he and his girlfriend were asleep, you snuck into their house, helped Hannah pack her clothes, put her in your car, and drove her four hours to a school of ministry in Kansas City."

He reiterated to me that somehow, while I was *in Alabama*, I had apparently *found* and silently *broken into* their house, packed her things, *persuaded* Marcus' girlfriend to leave her whole life behind and ride with me to Kansas City, and *enrolled her* into a school of ministry.

I had *never met* Hannah. I had *never even talked to her* before. I had no idea where their house was, and I hadn't even been to that part of the country in months!

Now, I'll be the first to tell you, I *don't* know what actually happened that night at Hannah's house. But I *do* know that after leaving Marcus and giving her heart fully to Jesus, Hannah finished ministry school in Kansas City and became a missionary. I *do* know

99

that, despite having lived through the horrors of addiction, abuse, and manipulation, Hannah is now a beautiful, vibrant young woman with a bright future ahead of her. And I *do* know that prayer is *powerful*—powerful enough to transcend time and space, to break social and spiritual bondage, and to move heaven and earth on our behalf.

As people of God's kingdom, we are not slaves to our location or our resources, though those things can certainly play a big role in the shaping of our lives. We are free. We are sons and daughters of the God of all good things, and we are dreamers to the core. As we learn to believe that His reach is much longer than ours and His pockets are much deeper than ours, we'll find ourselves dreaming a bit bigger, reaching a bit further, and we'll watch as the same freedom that has marked our lives begins to burst forth into the world around us, unleashing for them the same freedom He purchased for us.

Chapter 8

KATIE THE BLIND GIRL

One afternoon, I sat talking to Candice while she somehow managed—again—to do her makeup in the back seat of the van. We were nestled away at the far edge of a gravel parking lot in Oklahoma City as band members and venue staff worked around us like a hundred ants in a frenzy, each carrying their own equipment and setting up for the concert we had that night. The concert was in a bar. The other bands on the tour hated God, and weren't too crazy about us either. It was just another day at the office.

Suddenly, the sliding side door of the van was flung wide open and Mike (you remember Mike, he's the surfer guitarist who was shocked about my blackness, then came with me to get free food from nice Christians) stuck his head through the door with a big smile and wild eyes.

"You guys!" he shouted.

We were both a little startled. "Hey man! What's up?"

"There's a girl coming out here that we're gonna pray for," he said enthusiastically.

"Okay...," I replied, meaning it as more of a question than an answer.

He explained, "She's a friend of a friend, and she's blind. She wants prayer for God to heal her eyes."

"Oh wow...okay!" I said, trying to hide how intimidated I was. "Well... Let us know when she gets here!"

"For sure!" Mike said, slamming the door shut just as violently as he'd opened it.

Now, we believed in miracles. And when I say, "we believed in miracles," I mean, we'd read the Bible, and it seemed like miracles were a pretty common occurrence when Jesus was around. But, this was a *blind* girl. And, she was coming to *us* for help. What if we prayed and nothing happened? What if she wasn't healed? After a moment of fear and uncertain hesitation, I asked myself the right question: What if she *does* get healed? The thought filled me with a rush of excitement.

It can't hurt to try! I reminded myself optimistically. Remembering those silly W.W.J.D bracelets all the Christian kids used to wear in school, I thought, *What would Jesus do if a blind girl came to Him for help?* The answer was obvious. After all, it's not who *I* am that could help Katie, but who *He* is. So, I took a deep breath and settled it in my mind; we would pray for Katie, and we would see what God would do.

After a few minutes, Katie arrived with her friend. She was a pretty girl, with wild brown hair and fair skin. She wore a dark blue t-shirt, and smiled kindly—walking more confidently than any blind person I'd seen before. Mike, Candice, and I introduced ourselves and asked Katie if she would share her story with us. She obliged.

"I'm a Special Ed teacher for high school-aged kids with disabilities," she began. "A few months ago, while dealing with a situation in the classroom, one of our students head-butted me in the face and broke my nose. When my nose broke, small shards of bone broke off and were driven back into my eyes. As it stands right now, I am blind in one eye, and my vision is only getting worse in the other. My doctors have said that it will get progressively worse for me until I'm completely blind in both eyes, and there's really nothing that can be done to stop it."

"Wow!" I think we all said, trying our best to put ourselves in her position.

She continued to carry the conversation along for us, saying, "I know that you guys love God, so I thought maybe you could pray for me. I could really use a miracle."

Her simple faith touched my heart. As I heard her speak, I realized that I had been so concerned with *my reputation* that I had never really considered *her affliction*. I hadn't had compassion or love for Katie. I had, at my worst, been worried about how bad it might make me look if I prayed for her and nothing happened, and at my best, I'd been excited about how good it would make me look if I prayed for her and she actually *did* get healed.

I took a deep breath, let go of my self-concern, and allowed myself to see Katie through God's eyes. He just loved her. He wanted good things for her.

I smiled and said, "Well then... Let's pray!"

We came together around our new friend Katie, all laying our hands on her. Candice prayed first, powerfully acknowledging how valuable and precious Katie was to God, declaring the truth of God's Word for Katie, and reminding her of God's good and perfect plans for her life. She spoke to Katie's eyes, calling them back into God's original purpose for them—to behold His glory and to testify of His goodness.

Katie cried.

When Candice finished praying, we asked Katie if there had been any change in her vision. She blinked a couple times and gasped.

"I can see colors and shapes now in the eye I was blind in! It's definitely better!"

We were blown away! Any doubt or uncertainty I had was shrinking quickly, and I reminded Katie of one of my favorite promises God makes in scripture: "He who has begun a good work in you will see it through to completion."

I said, "Katie, the fact that God has *started* the work of your healing is evidence of His desire to *finish* the work of your healing! I believe it!"

"Me too," she said, with hope in her voice.

"Let's pray again!" I said to the group, and we gathered around Katie again.

With a fresh fire and reinforced confidence, we wrapped Katie up and prayed once again. She cried hard this time, her shoulders shaking at first as she tried to hold it in. After a minute or two, the weight of the moment seemed to have passed, so I said, "What do you think, Katie?"

Still crying, she took a moment to regain her composure and dry her eyes. As she did, she said to her friend, "Hand me your driver's license." He pulled out his wallet and handed it to her. She broke down in tears again and hunched over, putting her hands on her knees to keep from falling.

Between sobs, Katie said, just loud enough for us to hear, "I can see!"

We exploded into a wild circle of shouts and cheers. We cried and clapped and didn't care who saw us. Katie the blind girl could *see*! God had done something that even *we* could hardly believe!

We spent the rest of the night reeling from what we'd experienced. We had seen God's love for her in action. It changed something in all of us. Things we had once questioned or merely hoped for were now actual possibilities. We started to believe—I mean *really* believe—that anything was possible.

We caught up with Katie about two years later to find that she still has 20/20 vision. God wins. Again.

CAMILLE WAS A DANCER

Camille was a dancer. We met her at a concert in the back of a dark nightclub in North Carolina. She wasn't a dancer at that point; in fact, she was struggling to fold a t-shirt she had just gotten while clumsily leaning on her crutches. Candice saw her from across the room and felt drawn to her. Paying attention to that still, small voice, she left her seat and walked over to meet the girl.

Camille was a petite girl, maybe 19-years-old, with blonde hair that laid lightly on her shoulders. My wife approached her and, after helping stuff the t-shirt into her purse, Candice said, "Hey, if you don't mind my asking, why do you have to use these crutches?"

"Oh, it's because of my hip," she said. "A couple years ago, I was diagnosed with a form of cancer. My doctor put me on a specialized treatment, and the treatment caused my bones to deteriorate. The bones in my knee were almost ruined, so he had to remove bone from my hip and graft it into my knee."

"Oh my gosh!" Candice said.

"Yeah," Camille replied. "It's incredibly painful. The doctor says that I should be able to walk without the crutches in a few months." She looked down at the floor, hesitating briefly, then added, "But he said I won't be able to dance again."

Candice was a dancer for years growing up. Her heart was gripped, and the question of why God had drawn the two of them together had been answered. She welled up with love for Camille, and poured it out in the form of a simple question: "Can I pray for you?" Realizing how out of place that might sound, she explained, "We see God do wild miracles in peoples' lives often. Recently, we saw a girl regain vision in her blind eye. I just think God loves you, so I'd like to ask Him to take all of your pain away. If that's okay with you, of course..."

Camille kindly obliged, and bowed her head. Candice knelt down, giving little thought to discretion, and placed her hands on Camille's legs, then on her feet. She prayed with fervency, confidence, and power. She spoke first to the pain in her body and the decay in her bones, commanding them to leave. She spoke to the purpose and plan of God for Camille's life, and she called it into being. She declared *impossible* things for Camille, and she did so boldly, because she knows the God of impossible things.

As Candice finished, she stood up, collected herself, and asked Camille if she felt any change. Camille, pursed her lips and furrowed her brow with determination, put both her crutches in one hand, closed her eyes again, and took a step.

Immediately, her shoulders heaved, her blue eyes overflowed with tears and she began to sob. She handed her crutches to Candice and shouted, "I don't need these anymore!" Candice waved the crutches in the air, cheering wildly and causing a commotion in the venue. She didn't care. Camille walked, then ran, then *danced* back and forth across the room, half-crying and half-laughing.

We were overwhelmed! Camille had walked in to this dirty night club, expecting to stand around, just another spot in a sea of faces, leaning over her crutches and watching some metal bands play. In her heart, she was doing her best to cope with the reality that, though it had been a life-long dream of hers, she would never be able to dance again. Simply going about her business, she ran into Candice, and everything changed. Not just her day changed, not just her plans or expectations, but her *life!*

Camille came out to another show about a year later to update us on her life. She had walked into her church the next Sunday, walked tall down the middle aisle, and thrown her crutches down at the altar for everyone to see what God had done. Her doctor had never seen anything like it before. And, most unbelievable of all, she had enrolled in college...*as a dance major!* God restored the stolen dream to Camille's life, as He has done for so many others. Her heart was full, and her story still serves as fuel to our fire today.

Once again, God wins.

Chapter 9

SARAH, CANDICE, AND HOPE

The sweet freedom Camille experienced was only magnified by how familiar both Candice and I had become with the savage reality of cancer. When I was eight years old, I watched as it took my father's life—but not without robbing him of his strength and his personality first. My most vivid memories of my dad are of him being unable to leave his hospital bed, or even roll himself over. Of him gasping for air and being unable to speak. His death left my mother with the impossible task of facing her own grief while also walking through life with a violent, angry eight-year-old boy, and a confused two-year-old girl. I didn't realize it at the time, but my mom was a super hero.

Candice was familiar with the cruelty of cancer also. When she was five years old, her mother was rushed to the hospital after having a massive seizure. On a few occasions, she has recalled to me what she remembers of that night—sitting in the back seat of a family friend's car as they loaded her mom into an ambulance, watching and wondering what might happen to her family. Then, a few days later, she was told that during the tests and procedures, the doctors discovered a tumor the size of a baseball in her mom's brain. The treatments would cost their family hundreds of thousands of dollars, and take from them their mother's beautiful vitality, vigor, and energy.

Her mother's name was Sarah. And the first time I met her— 14 years after her initial diagnosis—she carried a gentle peace and sweet hospitality that I will never forget. The long, wavy, blonde hair I saw in pictures from years earlier had given way to shorter hair that was colorless and plain—a harsh reminder of the vicious reality of chemotherapy. The cancer had taken also her vision in one eye, so she wore wire-frame glasses with one lens fogged over. They were always a bit crooked, though no one ever said anything about it. She wore white tennis shoes that would squeak with every step as she walked gently across the vinyl floor of her kitchen. And her balance wasn't very good anymore, so she would sit and slide down the stairs one at a time when she needed to go down to the laundry room in their family's home.

Everything Sarah did was delicate. The only time I ever saw her lose her humble disposition was while yelling "Get him!" at the screen during an Alabama football game—an outburst she promptly apologized for, making us all laugh. I remember sitting to talk with her in her living room, her soft hands folded tenderly in her lap and her legs crossed with care. She had a wonderful ability to make you feel like you were the most interesting, exciting person she'd ever met. The truth is, she just loved to be with people, and people loved to be with her.

But after over 15 years of living with the hardships and limitations of her cancer, she was tired. At our wedding, she whispered to one of her closest friends, "I know Mattie will take good care of Candice. I'm ready to go now whenever God will take me." A few months later, the cancer began to spread again. She had one more surgery—a procedure the doctors performed in desperation—and we prayed. We prayed that God would give wisdom to the doctors, or that He would intervene Himself and miraculously remove the cancer from her body.

Nothing happened.

We had a big tour scheduled at that time, and Candice opted to stay home with her mom for this one. Some time later, as the cancer ran its course, I followed suit, leaving in the middle of the tour to be with my wife and her family. We prayed more.

Still nothing.

Then, one sunny afternoon in August, we stood at Sarah's bedside with the rest of her family, and we watched as what little life she had left was lifted from her body. Candice's dad wept as he was forced to let his wife go after 37 years by her side. That day we held on to each other a little tight, a little longer.

I think the strangest thing about it all was that, though our little world had come to a screeching halt, the rest of the world didn't seem to notice. The cars still passed by along the road out front, carrying people who were still hurrying to make their appointments. The TV was still broadcasting inane chatter about things that mattered much less than they once had. It was like our family had woken up one day to find that we were in a snow globe, forgotten on a shelf somewhere; sitting in tortured silence, watching the world go about business we now felt completely isolated from.

A few days later, I performed her funeral ceremony. I reminded those in attendance of the beauty of Sarah's heart, and I talked about God's goodness, even in the midst of tragic loss. I felt like a liar. If I was honest, I might have told everyone how confused I really was, and that I was angry with God. I didn't understand how (or why) the same God that healed the blind girl in Oklahoma and the dancer in North Carolina could ignore our plea for Sarah. I pretended to understand; I felt like Candice needed me to be strong, but I wasn't strong—I was wounded and discouraged. I didn't have an answer for myself, much less my wife in her grief.

But time, as it does, moved on. No matter how strange it felt, we were being dragged into the future, and we tried to get our feet back under us. We could have used our frustration to develop some strange belief about God that would accommodate disease, and loss, and death. We could have allowed our disappointment and loss to steal our faith from us (as it has so many others). We could have shrugged our shoulders and said to the broken and hurting world around us, "Sorry, but we can't help you. We've got problems of our own." To be perfectly candid, I think we tried those coping methods for a while, but they just didn't fit.

Eventually, Candice put on a brave face and came back on tour. I think it hurt more than she let on. It's a strange feeling to try to go back to the way things were, when you know in your heart that they will never be the same again. As time has passed, I watched her learn to live without Sarah, in the way someone learns to function after losing a limb. Things have never been the same, but she pressed on.

Since her mother's death, and even in the way she has struggled, Candice has taught me much about the unspeakable power of hope. She has shown me that *real* hope is able to reach up through the muck and mire of disappointment, and cling valiantly to the knowledge that the story is still being written. It's like a faint light on a distant shore; or like a familiar voice calling your name in the darkness. It reminds us that no matter how trying our present moment is, we are not too far from home.

If I'm honest with you now, I still don't understand. I don't know why the God of miracles is so evident in some situations, and seemingly distant in others. But I choose hope. And I believe that this hope is able to leap over my discouragement, to break through my doubt, and to carry me on as I sail through uncertain waters.

Though I may not always see what I hope for, I know God is able, and I know God is good. And sometimes, whether I like it or not, that has to be enough.

Chapter 10

ADVENTURES IN WALMART

Eventually, we got back into the swing of things after Sarah's death. We were on the road full time again, sharing our music and our hearts with anyone who would listen. The crowds were much bigger at that point. One night, we stood on a familiar stage—the same venue in San Antonio, where *two people* once came to watch us perform. This time, it was bursting at the seams, holding a capacity crowd of over 1,000 people.

After that concert, still buzzing from the excitement of the show, we all piled into the van and it lurched forward, rolling carefully out of the alley behind the venue. We drove through the night to Corpus Christi, Texas, for the next show. Sometime in the early morning we pulled into town, and as we have done often, we parked in the back corner of a local Wal-Mart to sleep for a while.

In the morning, Candice woke up sick. She had been feeling ill for the last few days—just exhausted and queasy. Gathering our things together, we snuck out of the van as quietly as possible, wiping the sleep from our eyes and adjusting our clothes. We started the day just like we did many others—by walking into a random Wal-Mart to brush our teeth.

We went through our usual morning checklist, enduring the awkward glances or comments that come when you prepare for your day in a public restroom. (I hope you never understand what I'm talking about.) That morning, though, Candice suggested something that shot through me like a bolt of electricity.

"I think I should go get a pregnancy test."

"Uh...what?" I asked.

"I don't know. I've been sick every morning for the last week, and I'm tired all the time. I think we should just check." She said, ever the reasonable one.

"Okay. Couldn't hurt to check, I guess." I replied, trying my best to stay calm.

We wove our way over to the pharmacy section and picked up a pink pregnancy test box. This was new ground we were covering, and nothing we thought of to say seemed appropriate, so we walked together in awkward silence. I held my breath as we checked out, and made our way back to the bathroom at the front of the store.

"Alright. Go get 'em!" I said, holding my hand up to give Candice a high five, trying desperately to hide the terror I was feeling.

She rolled her eyes and walked into the bathroom.

Eventually, after what I'm pretty sure was at *least* four hours, she came out. I couldn't read her facial expression, so I just stood there shaking like a guilty man waiting for the judge's verdict. She looked at all the random strangers walking around us and took a deep breath.

Finally, she looked back at me and said, "Well... Here we go."

My knees gave out, my stomach churned, my head spun wildly, and I leaned against a nearby chair to prop myself up. I had a million questions with no answers, the most pressing of which was: *Why did this have to happen in a Wal-Mart in Corpus Christi?* I see all these cute photos and videos of wives telling their husbands about their pregnancies, and they're all so beautiful and emotional. But in our story, we were both wearing sweatpants, and standing between a south Texas McDonalds and a dirty Wal-Mart bathroom. It was so very....*not* romantic!

I think it was a really good idea for God to give us nine months to prepare for parenthood. I was clearly not ready to be a father at that point, but over the course of the pregnancy I hyped myself up enough to at least be able to fake it for 18 years or so.

While we are on the subject, can you imagine how terrifying it would be if we *didn't* have that nine months to prepare? I mean, what if you got pregnant, and then woke up the next morning to go to the bathroom, and your new baby just plopped out onto the floor? Like, 'Boom. You're a parent now. Deal with it.' That would be the worst! Thank God that's not the case.

Anyway, back to the story at hand... Candice was pregnant. We were on tour with the band. We wandered aimlessly around Wal-Mart, both of us silently freaking out. Everything was changing, whether we liked it or not.

THAT TIME I QUIT THE BAND

After a while, I worked up the courage to tell the rest of the band our news. The conversation went about how I expected. We quickly moved through the obligatory congratulations and well wishes, before finally landing on the pressing issue: "So, what does this mean for the band?"

"Well," I said, "I think this means I'm done. At the end of this tour, I'm going to have to call it quits, and go find a real job to provide for my family."

A few moments of quiet discomfort passed, ending only when someone said, "Okay."

The thought of quitting made the next shows bittersweet. The idea of walking away from this wild adventure was a sad one, but I felt it was what had to be done. It was my duty as a man to be responsible, to leave this silly band, and to engage myself with matters of consequence. That's what a *real* man would do—or at least that's what I told myself.

A few days later, Candice and I sat eating dinner, escaping briefly from the strange rhythm of life on tour to pretend like we were a normal married couple. We discussed the future and the hopes and plans we had for the next part of our lives, and she asked me a question that stopped me in my tracks.

"Did God tell you to quit the band?"

I froze, squinting my eyes and setting my fork down. "I mean... I have always thought that if you got pregnant, I would have to move on." I answered, trying to sound mature.

"But, have you even *prayed* about it?" She continued. "You always say, 'We don't do the things that "just make sense," we do the things God calls us to.' Is this what God has called you to do?"

126

I stumbled over my words for the next few minutes, thinking out loud and trying to decide how I really felt about the situation. God *hadn't* told me to quit the band. Honestly, I *hadn't* really prayed about it. I'd been so shocked and scared by the news of her pregnancy that I had forgotten to ask God for direction at all.

All these thoughts ran through my head as I thought about how best to respond to her, eventually I looked up at her and said humbly, "I'm just scared."

"I know," she replied tenderly, in the way only a wife or a mother can. "But, the best thing you can do for our family is to hear the voice of God. Don't be scared. He *always* provides for us!"

After that conversation we started praying through the situation together, eventually coming to the truth that, as far as God was concerned, I was still supposed to be in this band. And, until He said otherwise, I would *continue* being in this band. Did it make sense? No. Was I comfortable with that decision? Definitely not. But God had been faithful to us to that point, so we thought it was a pretty safe bet that He'd continue to be faithful in the future.

Candice stood by my side as I humbled myself and gathered the guys in the band to admit my mistake. I told them, "I spoke out of turn the other day. I was afraid, and I made a decision out of fear, not faith. I always imagined that if Candice got pregnant, I would be done with the band. But now that we're really in that situation, I don't think it *has* to happen that way."

Over the next few days, we came together and developed a plan that would work for everyone. We would play a maximum of 120 shows each year. And, when we were on tour, we'd take one day off a week, and I could fly home to spend the day with my family.

It wasn't really how any of us imagined things going, but it would work. Candice's life would change the most. She would leave the road, laying down her passion to meet, pray for, and speak with new people each night, and she'd become the anchor that held our ship in place.

As we planned and prepared for this great transition into parenthood, the importance of "home" began to weigh heavily on us. Later that year, on September 17th, 2011, our first son, Kai was born. He was beautiful and perfect, and more than we could ever have asked for. We adjusted to the new life we'd been given, but as we did so, we began to realize that we hadn't yet known what home really was.

FINDING HOME

We had gone to churches before. At that point, when we weren't on tour, we went to services at a great ministry in northern Alabama called The Ramp. It was really a beautiful place, but it wasn't "home" for us. Something I'd read about years earlier had stayed with me, tapping me on the shoulder and constantly reminding me that there was more out there than I had yet to experience.

The author of this book recounted his pursuit of something he called "a spiritual father." He described a relationship that provided accountability, support, and direction in his spiritual walk. I'd had pastors before—as in, a guy I listened to on Sunday mornings, and other men I admired from a distance. I'd had teachers and authors I looked up to—people I learned a lot from, and aspired to be like, but I didn't have a *relationship* with any of these people. They didn't know me, I didn't really know them, and let's face it, there is only so much you can do to help someone you don't know.

I'd kept this desire for a spiritual father hidden in my heart for years. *For Today* had gotten much bigger than we ever expected at that point, and it was a bit intimidating for me. If I was going to handle that level of influence with integrity and humility, I knew I needed to have someone I could lean on—someone who could see past my job description and ask me the hard questions. There was no one in my life that would sit down and ask me how my marriage was going, or if I was making wise decisions with my finances. There was no one I could confide in about the pressures or responsibilities of ministry, and it was something I needed desperately then, more than ever.

So, I did something crazy. I asked God to bring that to person to me.

Shortly after Kai was born, a friend of mine called me out of the blue. He said, "Mattie, I was praying for you the other day, and I really felt like I needed to connect you with my spiritual father."

He'd told me before about this man; a man people called an apostle. I didn't know what that meant, but if it was a door God was opening, I was in. So I agreed, and told my friend I was willing to get together with the man.

We had a concert scheduled in Pensacola, Florida a few days later, which was close to where this man lived, so we made plans for the apostle to come by the venue and meet with me for a bit. I didn't know what to expect. I doubt he did either.

The evening came, and it was business as usual. Our gear had been loaded into the venue, we'd set up and sound checked, and we were ready to go on stage. I got a call, just minutes before we were scheduled to go on stage from a number I didn't recognize.

"Mattie? This is Aaron," said the deep, southern voice on the other end of the line.

"Oh, hi!" I said, pretending I didn't already know that.

"I think I just pulled up to the venue. Where can I find you?" he asked.

I told him, "I'm just on the side of the venue, under the street light."

I walked down the sidewalk a bit, away from the crowd, to meet him. As he walked up the street, we greeted each other with a manly handshake, and then a little less manly hug. I was nervous. I'd never met an apostle before. I still didn't know what that meant, but it sounded important.

Aaron smelled incredible. I know that's weird to say, but I can't describe him without mentioning it. He was a middle-aged man with tan skin, light blue eyes, and short, gray hair he wore combed straight back. He wore a blue Nike t-shirt, tucked tightly under his dad belly and into his jeans, and he carried a strange air of authority with him—not the kind of authority that intimidates and manipulates, but the authority that comes from really knowing who you are. He wasn't there to impress me. I appreciated that.

After chatting a bit, we went inside and I handed him some earplugs. He patiently stood on the side of the stage and watched our concert. Hundreds of sweaty kids climbed on top of each other to scream the lyrics of our songs with me. Generally speaking, this was not "church folk" territory, but he managed to make it through the entire set. He didn't stage dive, though we tried our best to convince him it would be okay.

After the concert, we went back outside of the venue. I was dripping with sweat and still out of breath, but we sat for a long time and talked. He thanked me over and over again for the opportunity to come to the concert. He told me that it had moved him and blessed him more than he could explain. We talked about the church in Mobile, Alabama, that he'd started 22 years earlier and pastored ever since. He was like a proud papa as he spoke about the awesome people in his congregation and how thankful he was for them, and he shared with me some of the dreams God had put in his heart.

Our time together that night wasn't anything spectacular. It was one of those moments that probably would've seemed pretty unremarkable to anyone else in the room. But as he spoke, I saw the heart of a real father. He wasn't just someone who loved to preach or wrote good books, he was someone who *loved people,* and was willing to lay himself down to see them succeed. I left that conversation with one very clear thought: *I wanted to go wherever Aaron was going*. He sent me a text message on his way home that night. After listening to a sermon CD I gave him and hearing my heart, he wrote and simply said, *We fit together*. I believed him.

Within two weeks, Candice and I had set a plan in motion to move to Mobile, Alabama, and join Apostle Aaron's church. It's the church we are still a part of today. It's a weird church, full of unique, vibrant people—from the skinny prophet lady with wild blonde hair who yells during sermons, to the awkward young adults who came because they liked my band, then stayed because they found their tribe. We're unapologetic about who God has called each of us to be, and we're thankful for what God has called all of us to become together.

My church family has taught me that "home" is not the church I attend, or the address on my driver's license, but the people I get to walk through life with. Home is the anchor that keeps me connected to the things that really count, no matter how far I go to answer the call of ministry. Home is where they see me for who I actually *am*, not the person they *think* I am—for better or for worse.

Over these last years, Apostle Aaron has gotten close enough to me to see some of my biggest faults, and he still hasn't gotten offended or given up on me. Instead he always calls me back to the standard, reminding me of the man I *can* be, even during times when I'm not really acting like it. He's a papa. He's always teaching, often correcting, and occasionally rebuking me. I'm thankful for him.

Maybe more than anything else, being in a relationship with Apostle Aaron and the rest of the incredible people at our church has taught me this: There's no such thing as a perfect church. Sometimes, the most incredible people can let you down or disappoint you. But, that is *exactly* why God calls us to "be one" with each other! There is no better way to develop the character of Christ than to remain committed to loving people who can disappoint, frustrate, or even offend you.

You know, they say, "home is where the heart is." I think that's true, but maybe in a different way than I had it explained to me. Home is not always where my heart *remains*, but rather where I can always go to find the heart that this world so often tries to steal. If you've lost heart, come home. If you've gotten lost in the cold unforgiveness of this world, the thing you're looking for is home. Find the people you can "fit together" with. That is where the heart is.

Chapter 11

"FOR TODAY HATES GAY PEOPLE"

Time went on and so did our lives. Toward the end of 2011, David

(our drummer), answered God's call to leave the band and step into

full-time ministry. Shortly after that, he moved to Ambato, Ecuador,

for two-and-a-half years to plant a church with a group of other

missionaries, and he has since started working with a group called

Extreme Nazarene to mobilize missionaries all over the world.

After David left, Mike's heart started moving in a new

direction as well. He had recently gotten married, and he was

beginning to dream a bit more often about what else might be out

there for him. After about a year of wrestling with and praying

about how and when he would leave the band, he shared with the

rest of us his plan to leave in the early summer of 2013, after one

last tour with us.

A few weeks before Mike's last tour was scheduled to start,

he addressed his online following about the apparent tightening of the government's grip on the application of Biblical Christianity, specifically regarding their treatment of churches and ministers who had spoken openly about the issue of homosexuality.

As is tragically common in our modern high-tech culture, Mike's comments reached far beyond the group to whom they were written, where they were met with confusion, disdain, and anger from many people in our scene who had spent a long time searching for a reason to hate *For Today*. We'd been known as "the Christian band" for a long time, but now they felt they had reason to label us "bigots," "homophobes," or "hatemongers."

The secular, largely anti-Christian news outlets that cover the hardcore/metal scene we are part of were more than happy to take Mike's statements out of context, to editorialize them to fit their "Christians are bad people," narrative, and to vilify Mike in the eyes of their following. When I first caught wind of what was happening, hundreds of thousands of people had already joined in on the movement against our band, and many more were still to come.

Things escalated rapidly, the issue became so inflamed that people were making videos of themselves burning *For Today* CDs and t-shirts, and several bands, managers, and booking agencies vowed publically to never work with our band again. People started organizing protests against our band at the shows on our upcoming tour, and calling venues and demanding they ban us from performing there. Some even went so far as to threaten our lives and our families.

Simply put, it was every band's worst nightmare.

Our business team was freaking out. I had people from our management company and record label calling and e-mailing me nonstop, begging me to do some "damage control," as they called it. Before I did anything, I called Mike to check in with him. He was obviously upset about the situation. He had not intended for anyone to be hurt or alienated by his statements. We talked for a bit about what we thought was best, both agreeing that the only option that allowed *For Today* to continue touring would be for him to step aside a few months early and skip the last tour he was planning to do with us.

It was a strange thing, seeing such an intensely ugly situation arise to cut Mike's time with the band short. While I hated that it had to happen that way, it ultimately was unavoidable. But even after the decision for Mike to leave the band was made, we still had to discern how to address the hundreds of thousands of people that had been left feeling hurt, victimized, or alienated by what they'd read about us.

WHERE DO WE GO FROM HERE?

After that conversation with Mike, I needed to address the concerns of the people who surrounded us in the music industry. Everyone from managers and booking agents, to other bands, music venues, record labels, music news outlets, and countless fans wanted to know—what did we have to say for ourselves?

I was torn. I wanted to support Mike. Mike was my brother, one of my best friends in the world. But I also knew that if I tried to explain, defend, or elaborate on what he'd said, no one would really hear me. People were furious and looking for a fight. And when people are looking for a fight, they'll never settle for a conversation.

I asked two people for advice that day, Candice and Apostle Aaron. They both said the same thing: Ask God what *He* thinks.

So, much to the confusion (and probably frustration) of some of my fellow band members, our manager, and our record label, I sent a short e-mail to everyone involved, and said, *I'm turning my phone off for the rest of the day. I'll have something to say tomorrow.* Then I took my family to the park, to remind myself what really matters.

I didn't know what I would do, but I had to trust that God was much smarter than me, and that he would help somehow. That night before bed, my wife and I got down on our knees, and with our fingers locked together on our soft, beige comforter, we prayed a very simple prayer. We asked God to get rid of every other voice that was trying to push or pull us in any direction, including our own. We asked Him to make *His* heart clear to us, and to give us wisdom to be able to move forward confidently. I fell asleep that night with Candice's arms around me, comfortable in the knowledge that God would be with me.

Early in the darkness of the next morning, with a shroud of sleep still laying lightly over me, I began to dream. In my dream, I could hear what I *knew* was the voice of God.

It said, "Do not defend what Mike said, and do not condemn what Mike said. *He* is not the issue—*they* are. Someone has to end this fight."

I woke up supernaturally clear and confident about what needed to happen. I was going to do something that even I couldn't have imagined. Everything in me wanted to defend myself, my friends, and my faith, but I would do the exact opposite. I decided to lay down my weapons, and get down on my knees in front of countless angry, hateful people, and simply say to them, "You can do your worst, but I will not fight with you."

That day, I released a video apologizing to anyone who felt like they'd been personally victimized or alienated by the things they'd read about us. I reminded them that, *all* are welcome where we are, regardless of religious or political beliefs, or sexual orientation. And at the end of the video, I gave them my phone number. *Really.* I got a second phone line turned on just for this situation, and I invited anyone who felt like they had something to say to call and to say it to me directly.

The reaction to the video was shocking. I think many non-believers were astonished to find a Christian who cared more about making peace than about arguing his point. So, they called. A lot. I woke up the morning after posting the video to over six *hundred* missed phone calls. I cleared my schedule, and did my best to talk with people as *thousands* of calls and text messages from around the world came in over the next week.

Mike hated the video. He called to tell me that it made him sick, and that he felt like I had let God down. Obviously, I disagreed, but I was too busy answering phone calls from people who'd been hurt or confused by what they'd heard about us to really pay much attention to his protest. I'd felt like we had been moving apart for quite some time, so I didn't try to stop the growing divide. It seemed the time had come for us to part ways, so I let it happen. I moved on with my life, and I let Mike move on with his, though I'm not particularly proud of this fact. I did a good job of justifying my dismissal of my brother for a long time, but I think it's important that I say this: You don't quit on family—no matter what. And, embarrassingly, that's exactly what I did to Mike.

All types of people called me over this issue. I spoke with everyone from pastors and Bible college students, to transgender people and drunk atheists. Some who labeled themselves Christians called to say how disappointed they were that I'd failed to "stand up" against the "liberal gay agenda." Some were homosexuals, calling to tell me how upset they were that I didn't condemn Mike's "homophobic" statements.

As many as there were that found a reason to be upset, there were still more that were really touched by the video. People called, from both sides of the *Christians vs. Homosexuals* debate, to say how challenging and refreshing it was to see someone at least *trying* to approach the issue with respect and humility. I had one lesbian girl call to thank me, saying, "I've never had a Christian stand up for me before."

It broke my heart. I was astonished to see how many people in our world have had only violent, angry, divisive images of Christianity from which to draw their conclusions. Most of them haven't met the kind, caring, revolutionary Christ followers that I have. They've seen angry conservatives on TV talking about how disgusting and perverted homosexuals are, and that's about it.

In our churches, we like to say, "Love the sinner. Hate the sin." But, if we're honest, I think we have to admit... *Most of us are much better at hating sin than we are at loving sinners.*

ONE CALL

In the midst of the unbelievable avalanche of phone calls, text messages, and voicemails, I answered one call that left me feeling utterly overwhelmed and shaken. My phone rang and the screen lit up, telling me that a call was coming from New Hampshire. I answered this one as I had hundreds prior.

"Hi, this is Mattie!"

The voice on the other end, seeming surprised that I'd actually answered, stuttered, trying to piece together a fitting introduction.

"Oh...uh... Hey..."

"Hey!" I replied with a laugh. "What's your name?"

"My name is Rory." Judging by his voice, I could tell Rory was a young man. He continued in a bit of disbelief, "Is this Mattie from *For Today*?"

"That's me!" I said with a smile. "What's up?"

"Oh man! I'm so glad you answered. After I saw your video, I wasn't sure if I'd actually get through, but I'm really glad I did! I just wanted to tell you my story, if that's okay." He seemed genuine in his desire to avoid being an inconvenience. "I really don't have anyone else I can talk to about it."

"Oh, of course," I reassured him. As you can tell from this book, I love to hear people's stories.

"Well, when I was born, my name wasn't Rory, it was Rosie," he started. It had just gotten serious. "I'm transgender, and I'm a Christian."

I have to admit, that was a sentence I had never expected to hear.

Rory continued, "A few years ago, after struggling with my identity for years, I was finally able to have my gender reassignment surgery. Right around that time, I met my girlfriend, Casey. She was a huge help for me, and she's been with me through a lot. Maybe about a year after my surgery, Casey asked me if I wanted to come to church with her. I didn't believe in God, but I thought it couldn't hurt to go.

"We walked into this church that she had heard about, and everyone was so nice to us. I sat there and listened to the pastor talk about Jesus, and at the end of the service, he invited people to come forward for prayer. I didn't know why at the time, but without thinking, I stood up out of my seat and walked to the front of the room. I didn't care who saw me or what they thought about me—I *needed* Jesus. I had an encounter with God that day that changed my life.

"Casey and I both gave our lives to God that day, and we started going to church together every chance we got. After a couple months, we signed up for their membership class, so we could learn more about the Bible and meet the pastor and everything. Eventually, they invited us to join a small group. It was awesome! The people there embraced us and welcomed us into their home, and they were so sweet.

"We all got to know each other pretty well, and eventually, I shared with them about my gender transformation. It was like I had flipped a switch. The people who had been so kind and welcoming to me began to pull back from us. They stopped inviting us to small group events, and would walk the other way when they saw us at church. Eventually, it got so bad I went to the leader of the small group to ask if I had done something to offend them. He told me, 'Well, it's difficult for us to know how to handle you, now that we know about your lifestyle. I mean, *we love you guys,* we just don't

agree with your lifestyle.'

"Eventually, it became so evident that we were unwelcome

there that we just stopped going. No one ever called to ask where

we went."

I was stunned. All I could blurt out was, "Rory, I... I don't

know what to say."

Rory started to cry. With a shaky voice, he said, "I have

prayed thousands of times for God to fix me, Mattie. What am I

supposed to do?"

My eyes filled with tears as well, and I managed to whisper,

"I am so sorry. I just don't know," before breaking down

completely.

Rory and I spent some time on the phone just crying

together. He cried because he'd felt the sting of rejection and

abandonment that can only come from people you've allowed

yourself to really trust. I cried because I realized how miserably we'd failed him and many others like him. In one moment, I'd come face to face with just how inadequate our sweeping generalizations and policies about marginalized groups of people really are. Those groups are made up of individuals, each with unique stories—many of them as heart-breaking as Rory's.

I had no answer for Rory's question. There's nothing about topics like this in the conservative Christian handbook. I simply apologized to Rory for anyone who ever failed to love him, and I promised him that, no matter what, Jesus never would. I begged him not to give up on Jesus, and then we prayed for each other—I for him, and he for me. We had very different struggles, and we saw life from very different perspectives, but we were family.

After our conversation ended, I was left alone with the harsh reality that I really *didn't* know how to answer Rory's question. What *is* he supposed to do? To be honest, I *still* don't know.

But I do know this: Rory does not intimidate God. No, instead God *loves* Rory, and God has an *incredible* plan for his life. And, if we claim to be people who follow Christ, we must—no matter how messy, inconvenient, costly, or confusing it may be at times—choose to see beyond someone's situation, and celebrate, identify, and invest in the inherent value they carry within them.

After all, no matter what situation, struggle, or circumstance has tried to identify or transform him, Rory is made in the image of the God we claim to love, just like we are. Right?

Chapter 12

A STREET FULL OF FRENCH HOOKERS

At one point, on a tour through Europe, we stopped for a concert in Lyon, France. Europe is a fascinating place to explore, so each day, I would leave the venue to go on an adventure through what seemed to me like another world. I took in architecture from ages long past, ate foods with names I couldn't pronounce, and smiled politely at the locals who would squint their eyes at me in curious animosity.

This day was a bit different. It was a sunny morning when I woke up and stumbled out of the tour bus. No one else was awake at that point, so I got myself together, and decided to go out for a while on my own. Lyon is a beautiful city! As I walked, I came first to a river that ran right through the city center, and I stopped and sat on its shore for a while, reflecting on all that had happened so far in Europe and all that might happen in the days to come.

After a few minutes spent watching little waves rise and fall, tumbling over each other on their way downstream, I decided to move on. I came back to the street and approached the next intersection, and as I did so, I saw a woman standing on the corner waiting for the light to change. As I got a bit closer, she turned to look at me, and I suddenly realized that she wasn't waiting for the light to change. She was waiting for someone—*anyone*—to hire her. The woman on the corner was a prostitute.

Maybe it was because it was 10 o'clock in the morning, or maybe it was because I only expected to see ancient architecture and buttery pastries on my walk, but the sight of a prostitute on the corner caught me off guard. By the time I realized she was a prostitute, we had already made eye contact; I was about ten yards away from her and closing fast. She looked me up and down, bit her lip, and made it very clear with her body language that she was "open for business" if I was at all interested.

My heart started to beat faster and my palms began to sweat. She really was beautiful. Her long, brown hair fell in perfect curls across her shoulders and her makeup was done well. She wore a silver skirt that was way too short and a pair of matching high heels that were way too tall. And she smiled invitingly as she looked right at me.

There was no chance I was going to actually hire this prostitute, but I have to be honest—it made me feel good to see how interested she seemed as I approached. I smiled slyly as I looked back at her, and I imagined how easy it would be, and how nice it would feel to have a night with a woman like that.

As I continued down the sidewalk and my moment of strange intoxication passed, I came back to my senses. Then I became sick to my stomach. I was ashamed of myself and disgusted at the thoughts I'd entertained about that woman. I was a *Christian* man, after all. A *married Christian man!* I had come there to France to share Jesus with people. But for a moment, it seemed, I had forgotten who I was, and it grieved me to think about how poorly I'd handled that situation.

I regained my composure after a few moments of mentally kicking myself, and continued to walk. I didn't have a destination in mind, I was simply strolling around Lyon to see what it had to offer.

After a few more minutes of walking, I turned a corner and saw a different prostitute standing on a different corner. I closed my eyes for a moment and took a deep breath. *I won't make the same mistake this time,* I promised myself, strengthening my resolve. I continued to walk, and I made sure to keep my eyes in check.

As I approached her corner, this prostitute noticed me and turned to get my attention, just as the other had. This time, though, I didn't look back at her. I didn't smile slyly. I kept my eyes locked on the pavement in front of me, and I didn't even think about the service she was offering. I clung tightly to my religious conviction, and managed to successfully pretend she didn't exist.

I felt much better about that scenario. I was pleased by my ability to resist temptation. I smiled and shook my head, thinking of how proud God must be of me for that. I reassured myself of my super-elite Christian status by thinking back over Bible verses I'd learned as a kid. Verses like, "Submit to God. Resist the devil, and he will flee from you." (James 4:7)

I continued walking around Lyon for an hour or so, and I passed dozens of other prostitutes. Sometimes my self-control prevailed, sometimes it faltered a bit. I never actually spoke to any of them, but each one I passed by, I considered either an object that existed to fulfill my desires, or a problem—a distraction from the important mission God had given me.

Eventually, I made it back to the venue we were playing that night, and as I sat, thinking back over the strange encounters I had that day, the great Holy Spirit confronted me with a devastating thought: I didn't *actually* care about any of those women. I didn't love them. I didn't see them as precious individuals who were made in the image of God, who had a destiny and a purpose, and who had had their brightest light stolen by a system designed to value only a small fraction of their whole being. Instead they were props—inanimate objects I had to step over to continue on with my righteous crusade. I didn't care that they were trapped in a profession that would destroy their souls. I didn't care that these girls—all of them daughters, sisters, or mothers to someone—were

157

so desperate that they would give themselves in the most intimate way to any man with a few minutes to spare and enough money in his pocket.

I called myself a Christ follower, but I had scornfully turned my nose up at people caught up in and hurt by sin, like I'd forgotten the value of the precious blood that was shed for them. I looked more like a Pharisee. I had forgotten that all people, *all people*, are made in the image of God.

I saw an ugly tendency in myself that many in the church have as well: I allowed people to become my *problem*, forgetting that they are actually my *purpose*.

Now, I may never lead a great revival in the Lyon, France, sex-trade community, but I could (and *should*) be able to at least look at those women with respect, and give them some dignity and honor in the way I think about them. I should be better than the perverts who abuse young women to satisfy their own desires, and I should be willing to look at them, no matter how uncomfortable it might make me, and acknowledge what has happened to them. I must have compassion. We, as Christians, need to be brave enough to see people through the eyes of love no matter where sin has led them, and as I wrestled with God that day, I made up my mind that I would do whatever I could to become that man.

A WARPED IMAGE

We spent the summer of 2014, performing on the main stage at the Vans Warped Tour. It was seven weeks of sheer insanity. Forty cities, 90 bands, 500,000 fans. It was absolute chaos! Each day, a team of hundreds would wake up with the sun to start the work, organizing and setting up stages, lights, sound systems, and hundreds of tents for food, clothes, music, and everything else you could imagine, only to tear it down and pack it up at the end of the night, so we could drive to the next city and do it all over again.

Warped Tour is a seven-week-long frenzy of insane heat, wild crowds, and unpredictable shows. The writhing sea of faces we stood on stage in front of were an eclectic and radical group. Some guys walked around in kilts and leather boots, some wore thick eye makeup and shirts adorned with pentagrams that said things like

"F*ck your God." Some girls just didn't wear shirts at all. It was a strange place. Certainly never boring!

The behind-the-scenes atmosphere was sometimes even stranger. Imagine taking 600 people—all actual rock stars in their own little world—and putting them together at summer camp. It came with all the new friendships and wild adventures we could expect, but also carried more weird social hierarchy and petty high school drama than we ever could have imagined.

We showed up to the first day of the tour looking for the guys we knew from other tours we'd been on. At first, everyone was just trying to figure out where they fit. Remember in high school, where everyone was urgently trying to find their place for fear that, if they didn't, they'd live the rest of the year as an outcast? That's exactly how it felt as we started our summer on the tour.

Even on day one, we members of *For Today* quickly realized that our reputation had preceded us. Some of the people on the tour knew us personally, but most didn't. Regardless, it seemed all of them knew that *For Today* was "the Christian band." That foreknowledge created a really interesting dynamic between us and the others involved with the tour. Sometimes we were met with hostility or uncertainty, but I think, most often, I would describe people's demeanor toward us as a pleasant indifference. Like, "Oh, *you're* the guy from *For Today*? I've heard about you guys…" They weren't upset or angry that we were Christians, just as long as our faith didn't infringe upon their fun.

And believe me, Warped Tour was all about fun. As insane as the days were, filled with crowd surfing fans, sweaty concerts, and lifelong memories, the party only intensified after the sun went down. All the business of the day was done, and a few hundred of the band members and crew would get together to rub shoulders, throw back drinks, and try to casually climb the social ladder.

There is this strange phenomenon in the music industry where friendship is rarely ever a genuine expression of someone's personality or desire, it's more of a business formality. You don't make friends on Warped Tour, you network. People will spend their entire summer desperately waiting for the chance to make friends with the hot new up-and-coming band, or the uber-popular singer—you know, the one with all the Instagram followers who all the girls go crazy for... We had friends, but we were still "the Christian band," so we didn't *really* have friends.

As the tour rolled on, and the late night after-parties and jockeying for social status continued, it became more and more obvious how poorly we fit in. I have a hard time with small talk and mindless banter, and in the tour world where friendships are mere formalities, that's about all anyone has to offer. People made polite, surface level conversation with us, most of them making a concerted effort to keep us at arm's length.

Occasionally, I'd bring up the topic of faith, curious to see how people would react. They would invariably tell me how much they respect me for my beliefs—sometimes in sort of a condescending way, like when a parent pretends their kid is really good at singing, to avoid hurting their feelings. They'd tell me how much they admire my devotion and wish they had the strength to live like me. It's a paper-thin shield I've seen countless times, thrown up in desperation to keep me from pressing an issue a person isn't prepared to face.

I didn't press, I just watched. I watched as guys I called friends began to avoid eye contact with me, for fear that they'd miss an opportunity to snag a selfie with Austin Carlile (he's *so* dreamy!). I watched as people I'd made small talk with for weeks snuck away again and again to feed their cocaine addiction, or stumbled drunkenly back into the shadows of the night, heading to their bus with a different girl than the one they'd taken to bed the night prior.

It was strange to see people spend so much of themselves on such hollow things. I don't think anyone really *liked* living their lives networking instead of connecting, or fighting for a little piece of the spotlight, but they did it anyway. They were starving for a real relationship, but each day, I watched as they settled for some drunken selfies and a one-night stand. It was heartbreaking. They were trapped; and anyone who had a different idea about the purpose or priorities of life was shunned. That's not to say they didn't agree with the ideas and ideals of Christianity or clean living, but they just couldn't afford to risk the social status they'd fought so hard to attain.

TREASURE IN THE FIELD

About a month into the tour, I sat on our bus, reading my Bible and I found something that completely revolutionized my approach to life. I was reading Matthew 13, and came across a familiar passage. In Matthew 13:44, Jesus says to his disciples,

> The Kingdom of heaven is like a treasure hidden in a field, which a man found and hid; and for joy over it he goes and sells all that he has and buys that field.

I'd heard that passage before. I think I remember reading it in Sunday school as a kid, my pastor teaching us that we must give *everything* we have to truly receive the Kingdom of God. He probably summed it up by giving us a cool, relevant Christian catch phrase like, "You gotta be all in for Jesus, guys!"

But as I read that passage on that day, God began to unwrap it in a way that has changed the way I view people forever. The first

164

thought I had was, *Why is it significant that the treasure was 'in a field'?* I mean, Jesus goes out of his way to explain *where* the treasure had been hidden. Was there something significant about that?

No sooner did I entertain that question than the answer erupted out of my heart. I thought about the other times Jesus talks about fields. He says, "Lift up your eyes to the *fields* for they are white for the harvest" (John 4:35). And, "Ask the Lord of the harvest, therefore, to send out workers into his harvest field" (Matthew 9:38).

When Jesus talks about a "field," he is talking about *people.* As I considered that reality, I looked again at Matthew 13:44, only this time, I saw it in a completely different context.

Where was the treasure hidden? In *people!*

As I explored that thought, another arose right on its heels: *If the field represents us, then who was the man walking in the field?*

I felt God begin to smile.

It finally dawned on me. In this passage, Jesus is telling the story of humanity's redemption! The man walking in the field was not *me*, it was *Him*! The Kingdom of Heaven is like a treasure hidden *in the hearts of* human kind, which...though most did not even *believe* it was there, Jesus saw. And, being overjoyed at the beauty He beheld (the beauty He *created*), He walked up Calvary's hill toward the Cross, and with His own blood, He gave everything He had, and He bought that field!

Something like waves began to crash down upon me over and over again. The thought of *treasure* locked away, hidden in the hearts of humanity, was beautiful but overwhelming. I remembered those French prostitutes. There was *treasure* in them I had failed to see, because I was so preoccupied by their job description. I thought of the people I'd seen all around me on Warped Tour— people who openly hated God, drug addicts, or the broken girls who would do anything to get the attention of a band guy. There is *treasure* inside them. All of them! As ugly as that culture could

166

seem, I began to realize that there was more beauty that I'd ever imagined inside each of these people.

When I looked at the prostitutes on that street in France, I saw their clothes and their job description. I never saw the treasure inside them. There was a wealth of creativity, and a vibrant beauty locked inside their hearts and covered over by the dirt of their circumstance. I hadn't taken the time to appreciate the work of art God had created when He formed each of them with His own hands. That art, so often muddied and twisted by sin's presence, is the *treasure* hidden in the field!

It dawned on me (probably much too slowly), that for *years* of my life as a Christian, I had viewed and valued people by their sins and shortcomings. In my mind, I would put a big stamp on their forehead that said something like "WHORE," "ADDICT," or "PERVERT." I knew God loved them, but if I'm honest, I didn't. I thought that they could maybe *become* special, but as things stood in their sinful lives, they had nothing to offer.

Suddenly, I started to look at things from Jesus' perspective. Something inside me began to wake up, and as I looked at people, "whores" became princesses who were still fighting to find themselves; "addicts" became revolutionaries, just waiting to find their cause. As God's heart began to grow inside me, I became more excited about people's treasure than I was intimidated by their sin.

People weren't disgusting or disappointing anymore, they were *dirty*; like a treasure buried in a field. And that was something I could relate to. I know what it feels like to be dirty. But I couldn't stop one thought that kept running through my head: gold is still gold, even if it's buried in dirt. The value of a person doesn't change based on their status or their struggle. There is a treasure inside them that is *so* significant, and *so* beautiful, that our Jesus—the one we so love to sing about and celebrate—considered it a *joy* to give everything he had to pay the impossible price so that He might finally have the treasure that has, for far too long, remained hidden in the field.

May God raise up a church on the earth who can see the treasure that has been forgotten or ignored by others. May we be undeterred by the layers of unbelief, sin, and shame that so much of the world wears proudly. May we become a people of relentless love. Relentless because we see a deeper value. An eternal beauty. A hidden treasure.

Chapter 13

RIGHTING WRONGS

As I began to see the treasure inside of people, I realized two things: First, there really *is* a treasure inside of every single person I'll ever meet. Second (and this one hurt a bit to admit), I had a tendency to ignore those treasures. Sometimes, I would ignore it because I was too busy to really see them. I mean, I would look at them, but I wouldn't really *see* them.

Sometimes I would ignore it because I felt like they were too dirty or broken for me to help. And sometimes, I would ignore it because I was too afraid to get in their dirt with them. Maybe I didn't want to deal with the burden or inconvenience of it, maybe I felt like I had better things to do... But, if we're being candid here, it was because I didn't really love them. I know that's not a very Christian thing to say, but it's the truth. Sometimes I don't love people. It's not like I want bad things for them, but sometimes I convince myself I don't have the time or the energy to really love a person, so I ignore them instead. And, let's face it, some people take more energy to love than others.

In the midst of the storm we endured after Mike's public comments and the backlash we faced from the gay community, my relationship with Mike ceased almost immediately. He and I had a couple conversations later that week, which basically consisted of him listing off the things I'd done wrong, while I desperately tried to explain myself to him. It didn't take long for us both to realize we were going nowhere and to stop trying altogether. Other than the occasional blog post about my failures as a minister and a Christian, I didn't hear from him after that.

Over the next years, I genuinely sought to forgive him for the damage he'd caused, and to take the "high road" in regard to his public attacks on me and my ministry. I prayed for him and his family. As they came to my attention from time to time, I made it a point not to acknowledge his comments, and to simply keep my shoulder to the plow; to do the work God had set before me, and not allow anything to distract me from it. My plan was going well until January of 2016, as I was reading a passage in Matthew 5 in which Jesus says the common Christian phrase, "Love your enemies."

The big problem I had with this was that, even after *years* of praying for Mike, blessing him with my words, and doing my best to move on emotionally, when I read the word "enemies," his face still popped into my head. He was the one I thought of when I thought of an enemy.

That really bothered me. I prayed silently, "God, I have forgiven him. I don't harbor any ill will toward him or his family. He is not my enemy!" But almost immediately on the heels of that prayer came the thought, *But I am his enemy.*

The weight of this sudden realization fell on my shoulders as I finally faced a truth that I'd been doing my best to avoid for years: I had made a decision in the chaos of that moment toward the end of Mike's time with us that I *knew* he would be unhappy with. I *knew* it would hurt and embarrass him, and I also knew that he'd want to confront me about it. Whether my decision not to publically support his statements was right or wrong was no longer the issue in my heart, the issue in my heart was simply that my brother was hurting, and I'd bailed on him. In the moment I *knew* he'd need family the most, I pulled back and let him go, because I didn't want to get my feelings hurt. On the heels of this realization, a truth shook me: Jesus says, "By this, the world will know you are my disciples; if you *love one another."(John 13:35)* I had been so concerned with loving the world that I'd refused to love my brother. And according to Christ, my love for my brother is the primary evidence of my association with Him!

I sat in my room with salty tears rolling down my cheeks as I realized just how miserably I'd failed to love my brother. I was ashamed. I was embarrassed. I was sorry. So went to my drawer, and pulled out a piece of paper and a pen. I sat down and began to write. I wrote a letter to Mike and his wife Susanna, simply asking them to forgive me for not being there for them during a time that must have been incredibly painful. I acknowledged that I'd been a coward in my dealings with them toward the end of our relationship, and that, in my fear of the "mess" our friendship might have been, I chose to simply end the friendship, instead of walking through the mess with them.

I told them that's not what family does. Family will stick it out with you through the pain, and through the mess. Family will fight for you even if you tell them not to. Family will hold you when you're hurt—even if they're the one who hurt you. Family isn't always perfect, but family doesn't quit. And I had quit. I'd failed to treat Mike like family.

But, where I failed years earlier, Mike succeeded. He and his wife graciously forgave me for pulling back from them, and together we celebrated the beauty of brotherhood and the goodness of God to return to us what we lost in our youthful pride.

Since leaving the band, Mike has learned two languages, been a youth pastor at a well-respected church, written three films, and now directs an NGO relief organization that provides expanding medical care for over 10,000 Kurdish soldiers in the Middle East.

I learned from my time with Mike that love really is all we have. I traveled around the world and reached millions of people with the Gospel during the years after Mike's departure. But still, in my heart, I carried with me the shame of having failed to love my brother in his time of need. There is no freedom greater than the freedom we feel as we surrender fully to Love—and to Love's desperate pursuit of our hearts. It might get messy, it might even hurt, but I promise you...in the end, it'll always be worth it.

MARCELA

I really believed what I'd learned about the "treasure hidden in the field." And as I allowed that idea to go deeper and do its work in me, my heart became much more tender toward the people I met. It changed the way I thought about others and the way I spoke to them. It was a revolutionary idea for me. I learned to look past peoples' fears and failures, and to look through God's eyes for the beauty inside them. I recognized that God was the one who put that beauty there—He'd built it into them, and I started to love to identify those beautiful things as I'd speak with people and help hold up a mirror so they could see the fingerprint of God in their own lives.

As I began to put this new philosophy to work, I started to see the incredible things that could happen when people discover God's treasure in their own hearts. As I would speak with people — whether they believed in God or not—I would do my best to see and to acknowledge the beautiful, unique gifts and traits He had given them.

Some people came alive when I'd tell them what I saw in them. Some people felt awkward and acted like they were suspicious of me. I think one of my favorites was Marcela. Marcela came to a concert of ours in New York City. She took the subway across Manhattan hours before we played to make sure she'd get a chance to meet us. As she approached me, she did so with such timidity that I wasn't sure I would actually get a word out of her. She was a short Hispanic girl, with long black hair pulled back into a ponytail that hung down her back. She hunched her shoulders a bit, and kept her eyes pointed toward the floor, like she was always afraid of being yelled at.

Hoping to shock her out of her shell, I smiled as wide as I could without seeming like a crazy person, and said, "Hey! How are you doing?"

"I'm good," she replied sheepishly.

I figured at that point I may have to carry the conversation. I held my hand out to shake hers and said, "I'm Mattie. What's your name?"

She followed my lead. "I'm Marcela."

"Well, it's really nice to meet you, Marcela! Thank you for coming to the show today!"

"Oh, thank *you* for coming to New York!" she replied as she handed me a poster to autograph for her.

As I signed it, I asked her, "Hey Marcela, do you follow Jesus?"

She looked away awkwardly and responded, "Well... No, I don't really believe in God," quickly adding, "But, I think it's cool that you guys do!"

I stopped for a moment before handing the poster back to Marcela. I wanted to take the time to *really* see her before our conversation ended. As I looked at her, it was like I could feel the love of the Father for her welling up inside of me. After a few seconds, I couldn't contain it any longer and I blurted, "Marcela, God *loves* you so much!"

She smiled politely and nodded her head to acknowledge that she'd heard me.

"No, I mean he *really* loves you!" This time though, I didn't stop there. I locked eyes with her and spoke with insight and confidence I knew could only come from God. "He loves you more than you could possibly imagine, and I think you know that! The abuse you suffered wasn't at the hands of God, but at the hands of godless people!"

I was way out on a limb at that point. I didn't know *how* I knew, but as I looked at her, it was like God was showing me the hurt, betrayal, and pain she kept locked inside her heart.

I continued, talking to the top of her head, since she'd ducked her face down, saying, "God's heart was broken by the evil that was done to you just as deeply as yours was. I think you know there is a God, and I think you know that He loves you. I think you're just too scared to let yourself believe again. Marcela, the people who hurt you have already stolen so much of your past— don't let them have the hope of your future as well!"

I spoke very boldly and freely about what I saw when I looked at Marcela. I'd forgotten about the long line of people standing behind her, waiting for photos or autographs. I wasn't quite sure how she'd react to all that until she looked up from the ground and I saw tears beginning to well up in her eyes. She took a step closer, leaning in to make sure that only I could hear what she said next, and she spoke softly.

"The abuse started when I was seven years old, and it was at the hands of my family members. I felt so dirty and I started to hate myself. Eventually, I worked up the courage to go to my parents about it, but they told me to keep it quiet—they didn't want to get the police involved because it would tear the family apart. So it just continued. No one did anything to stop it until I got old enough to move out."

As I heard her story, it was like I could feel her pain. My heart overflowed with compassion and sorrow for her, and I wrapped her up in my arms. For a long time, I just held her there, her arms around my waist as she cried into my chest. I invited her to forgive her abuser and to release the burden she held in her heart, and we held hands as she prayed to ask God to forgive her and heal her, and to forgive those who had hurt her. I watched as the weight of hatred and trapped pain left her and a great, glorious relief took its place. It was, I think, a transformative moment for both of us.

After a few moments, she collected herself, and I watched as the treasure hidden in her began to appear before my eyes. It was like a light bulb came on and she suddenly asked, "Do you think God could use me to help other people like this?"

"What do you mean?" I asked, not quite sure if I believed what I'd just heard.

"Well, I think there are other people out there who have been abused. Maybe I could help them find God and forgiveness too!"

A smile spread across my face. "Marcela, I'm *sure* of it!"

I told her about a promise of God that I've kept very close to my heart through the years. "God is able to work all things together for good for those who love Him and are called according to His purpose." (Romans 8:28). I told Marcela that, somehow, God could take the painful, ugly, horrible things that had happened to her, and use them for *good*. I told her something I'd seen proven more times than I could count: If she would let Him, God could make a beautiful future out of an ugly past.

Abuse is a dirty thing. It can harm not only the body, but it can also poison the soul. The beauty of Marcela's heart had been marred by the violence of the abuse and abandonment she'd suffered at the hands of those she should have been able to trust. Her treasure had been buried by the "dirt" in which she'd lived; but as Jesus got involved in her life, the dirt and disappointment of her past began to melt away, and her beautiful, compassionate heart began to shine through! Marcela came alive at the thought of being able to help hurting people, and realizing that her greatest struggle could become her greatest asset, if she would simply place it into God's hands. When she finally met someone who cared enough to face her "dirt," Marcela found the courage to stand up and face it herself.

Marcela went home from our concert that day and reestablished contact with her family. She shared the Gospel with her abuser and forgave him for the harm he'd caused, inviting him to commit his life to Christ as well.

She later said to me, "I won't put myself in a dangerous situation again, but it feels so good to be free from the bitterness and anger I held inside."

I saw Jesus wipe away the dirt that had been used to bury the treasure hidden in Marcela's heart, and show the world what had been hidden for years. It was beautiful—a different kind of beautiful than anything I'd ever seen before. I watched Marcela begin to step into the place she was supposed to be all along.

MATT THE FRENCH SINGER

A French band called *Novelists* landed the opening slot for our European tour in the spring of 2016. We shared a double-decker bus with the two other bands on tour, so Matt, the lead singer, and his band, rode along with us for a few weeks. As is to be expected, they took a few days to feel us out. They had moved into a bus with 12 strangers from the other side of the world, so they were naturally a bit timid.

As the days rolled on, I think they started to realize that, despite our differences in faith or nationality, we still had a lot in common. We made it a point to help them however we could—to accommodate, celebrate, and promote them—and they slowly let their guard down. We became friends. We made fun of their accents, and they tried to teach us French, then laughed at how silly we sounded.

Late one night, after playing a concert in Germany, we were driving through the rolling hills of Europe's heartland. I sat in the dim orange light and red leather chairs of our bus's lounge, typing away on my computer, muscling through the first draft of this book. As I sat there, Matt came down and sat across the aisle from me. Matt was a wild-eyed 24-year-old that spoke English with a funny French accent and had a sweet smile that shined through his shaggy beard. His wiry frame swam inside his extra-large t-shirts and his stretched earlobes wobbled back and forth when he laughed, which he did often standing out on the sidewalk with a baseball cap turned backwards on his head and a cigarette between his fingers.

He opened his laptop, popped in some headphones and started working on a project of his own. After some time, he looked up and caught my eye. He pulled one headphone out of his ear and I asked him, "What are you working on?"

"Leewicks," he said in his funny French accent. "We're working on a new album, and I'm listening to the songs, trying to come up with lyrics."

"Oh cool!" I responded.

"Yeah. It's very hard," He confessed, taking his headphones out altogether and readjusting himself in the seat. "It's hard to write lyrics that people want to hear."

Closing my computer to give him my full attention, I asked, "What do you mean?"

He answered, "Well, I want to write about my life. But to be honest, my life is "*sheet*" (French accent), so all my lyrics come out very sad and dark, so I don't know what to do."

I nodded my head, trying to come up with something appropriate to say, but he quickly continued, "I really like your lyrics. They are so inspirational. How do you write your lyrics?"

What an opportunity! I said, "Well, let me ask you this, Matt, do you have hope?"

"What do you mean?" he asked.

"I mean, you mentioned that your life is not good. But, do you have any hope that it might get better—that things could change for you?"

"I don't know," he said, his eyes darting back and forth.

I continued, "Because there's nothing wrong with acknowledging the hardship you've faced or the situations you've come through. But, if you have no hope, you have nothing to offer anyone!"

He seemed to really start searching his heart. I said, "Matt, you know my hope is in Jesus. And because of that, I know that, no matter *what* I face, He will carry me through. And, that is the hope I offer to people through our songs."

He took the conversation in a very different direction. "I see your hope. I see how you are always smiling and full of joy. And I watch you on stage every night, and you are so passionate about your message."

A smile crept across my face. "Yeah, man. It's because I have a message worth being passionate about!" Then I had to ask, "Matt, do you know God personally?"

"No," he replied. "I don't really know what to believe. I've never been to church or anything. My grandma was a witch. She's the only person in my family that had faith in anything."

I told him, "Matt, there is a God. He created everything, and He loves *you*. He has a dream for your life that is so far beyond anything you've ever even imagined that I couldn't explain it to you if I tried! And, He doesn't just invite you to believe in Him, He invites you to *walk* with Him—to have a real, living relationship with Him!"

Matt pursed his lips and said something I've heard countless times. "I don't know, man. I have really made a lot of mistakes in my life. Maybe I will find God someday when I can figure things out."

I pressed him, "Matt, God doesn't just want you to know about Him, He wants you to know Him. This thing is not about just reading an old book and trying to do what it says, it's about connecting with the God of the universe!" I continued, "I know you feel like you're too dirty to deserve God's love, but Jesus died to make you free from your sin so that you wouldn't have to feel dirty anymore! If you want to start a relationship with God, you don't begin by being more pious, or more studious, but by being forgiven!"

"Wow..." Matt said thoughtfully.

"If you search your heart, I'll bet you'll see that, more than any other thing, you're longing for *forgiveness*. To be made clean from the mistakes of your past, and to have the assurance of a beautiful new future!"

"Yeah," Matt said.

"Is that right?" I asked.

Something clicked in his heart. I could actually see a *visible* change in him happening right in front of me.

He said, "Yes! I really think I need this." He searched for words for a moment before adding, "I really want to know God and be forgiven."

I reminded him that, because of what Jesus had done on the Cross, he could be forgiven if he'd only ask, and that the door had been opened for him to speak with God *directly.* I asked if he'd like to pray with me, and he agreed enthusiastically. I prayed first and thanked God for the amazing thing that He'd done in Matt's life. Matt started to pray in English for my sake, and I said, "You can pray in French. Just pour your heart out to God—ask Him to forgive you, and know that He will!"

He prayed something I didn't understand, with passion and tenderness in his voice, then he looked up at me with tears in his eyes and a smile on his face.

"How do you feel?" I asked.

Matt took a deep breath and replied, "Amazing. I have never felt anything like this before."

Curious, I pressed, "What do you feel?"

He said, "It feels like... peace. I feel peace in my heart. I have never felt it like this before. I know I am accepted by God. And it feels like this is what I have always been looking for!"

We cried and hugged, then we laughed and thanked God for answering our call. As many times as I'd seen it, I was still overwhelmed to see the God of all creation visit us so freely and powerfully—awakening hearts to His voice and showering us with His love. He's just really very good to us.

Matt and I spent a lot of time together on that tour. We went on many late night walks through dark European streets, talking about the kingdom, the Bible, and the goodness of God, and exploring what it would mean for him to truly pursue God fully. One day, before the tour ended, he excitedly pulled me aside to say that he'd shared his experience with his girlfriend back home in France who confessed to him that she had also been seeking something "more" in life, and that she wanted to put her faith in Jesus as well, and begin a new life with Him.

The skinny, rough looking boy from France finally found the hope he'd once been so desperate for. The treasure in His heart— once buried by the disappointment and failures of his past—was now shining freely for all to see. I still stay in touch with Matt. He's doing so well, and I am very excited to see the great and wild adventure God will take him on next.

Chapter 14

CHANGE IS IN THE AIR

You know, words have power. We're all familiar with the dreadfully inaccurate old adage, "Sticks and stones may break my bones, but words can never hurt me," but the truth is, words *can* hurt. The words we choose can give life to the soul, and they can take it away as well. They can be profoundly illuminating in their effects, or be utterly devastating, even if they're not spoken with harmful intent. Think about how heavy the words, "Will you marry me?" might feel as they land upon your ears. Or, "I'm pregnant."

It was that type of heavy feeling I carried the night I sat down to tell my best friends, "I think it's time for me to leave the band."

We'd been on tour in North America for a few weeks early in 2016 when the whole thing just started to feel...different. I'd stood on stage in venues and performed concerts like the one on our tour thousands of times. But now, something about it began to feel strange. I wasn't sure exactly how it was different or how to describe the change for a while, but as I discussed it with my wife on the phone one evening, I said, "This just doesn't feel important to me anymore."

Those words stopped me in my tracks. I remembered days past in which I stepped out onto that stage with the full-hearted sense that what we were doing was eternally significant. It felt like destiny every single night. I *knew* that because of what we were doing, people would have their lives changed forever. But it just didn't feel like that anymore. It felt more like an obligation than an honor.

I asked Candice to pray with me for clarity. I wasn't sure if what I was feeling was because the *tour* had changed, or because *I* had changed. I went to God and laid my heart before Him, saying, "If my heart has grown cold for the ministry you've called me to, please change it. Make *me* passionate about what *You* are passionate about!"

After a few days of praying, a sobering thought found its way into my heart: The issue wasn't with me, it was with where I was. Now, don't get me wrong, I love performing with the band! There is nothing in the world like it, and nothing in the world like the amazing guys in *For Today* that I've been honored to perform with. But it felt like, for the first time in our career, I didn't have anything more to look forward to.

And *that* was it, I realized. We'd done it all.

As I thought and prayed and talked through what I was sensing, I realized that the feeling I had was not that God was shouting, "Mattie, get out of the band right now!" as if something about it was dreadfully out of line, but that the Father had sat back with pride in His eyes and His hands folded in His lap, and said softly, "Well done." The sense I had in my heart was simply that we'd done what we'd been sent to do. Our job was finished. And because of that, it was time to move on to what was next.

DROPPING THE BOMB

I spent days (or maybe weeks), trying to wrap my head around the seriousness of this decision before finally mustering the courage to talk to the rest of the guys. Toward the end of the tour we were on, when we were all in a hotel, I took advantage of what might be my last quiet moment with the whole group. I walked down the deep red hallway carpet to the room the rest of the guys were hanging out in, and held my breath as I knocked on the door. I walked in and sat down on the counter, and looked around at a very normal (for us) moment. Some of the guys were on their computers, some were watching TV, and some were unpacking. I was about to make things very awkward.

I got everyone's attention and talked fast before I lost my nerve. "Guys," I said, "I wanted the chance to talk to you all together. I've been praying about this for a while now, and I think it's time for me to leave the band."

Yup, awkward. And silent.

"Uh... I love you guys a lot, and I'm not, like, unhappy in the band or anything. No one did anything wrong," I continued, suddenly realizing how much this felt like breaking up with a girlfriend after 10 years of dating. "It's just... I know it's what God is calling me to do."

They were really kind and gracious, as usual. Brandon spoke up. "Well, if that's what God is calling you to do, then it's going to be great!" (Brandon's the guy you want around when you're in a stressful situation; he's the one who will always remind you that everything is going to be alright.)

"I'm sure there's a lot of stuff to figure out, but we can do that later. I just needed to tell you what's going on. So...yeah... I just love you guys a lot."

"We love you too," Ryan said.

I left the room so they could speak freely, plugged in my headphones, turned on some worship music, and danced in the hotel parking lot for the next hour. You want to know why? Because

God is good. And even in awkward, scary, life-changing situations, He STILL deserves my praise!

WHO AM I?

It's funny, I've given almost ten years of my life to this platform of music. While I was in *For Today*, I learned how to preach and pray, I met my wife, we had two babies, and we traveled all around the world. It's been the context for almost all of my adult life, but the prospect of leaving it behind doesn't scare me at all. I always imagined it would, but now that I'm here, facing this change, it really doesn't.

Years ago, just a few months after I joined the band, a mentor told me, "Never become Mattie from *For Today*." He explained, "You can be Mattie the Christian, or Mattie the husband, or Mattie the father, or Mattie the friend, but never become in real life who you pretend to be on stage."

That didn't really make sense to me when he said it, because at that point in time, the name "Mattie from *For Today*" didn't mean much to anyone. But that advice has become more and more important as the years have passed. I've realized that there is always a pull in the heart of a man to identify himself by his performance. To believe the old lie that our value is defined by our production. And that somehow, the man with the biggest platform can give God the greatest glory. Those things couldn't be further from the truth!

Glory and fame are not synonymous. The spotlight of fame shines on the wicked and the righteous alike, but there is no real glory to be had there. I've seen countless people chase a bigger and bigger spotlight, seeking the fulfillment that I *know* can only come from true glory—*God's* glory, and His calling for each of us to participate with Him in His plan. "For My thoughts are not your thoughts, nor are your ways My ways," says the Lord. "For as the heavens are higher than the earth, so are My ways higher than your ways, and My thoughts than your thoughts." (Isaiah 55:8-9)

With the band and its platform growing, it might not make sense from our human perspective for God to call me away from it.

But He has. And for His glory, I will go where He calls, trusting that He knows much better than I do.

LOOKING FORWARD

Now I sit and reflect on these last years of my life. The victories and defeats, the many lives we have poured ourselves into, and the overwhelming satisfaction that has come from it all. I remember the pain of disappointment, and the incredible joy of the countless miracles God did in us and through us, and I wonder, *Who will carry this torch? Who will say "yes" to the invitation of God to proclaim the Gospel in their workplace, just as we have done in ours? Who will rise up each day determined to do His will, and refuse to be ashamed of what He's done for us? Who will the Lord of the Harvest send to the field to find the treasure the world ignores?*

As I've grown older and maybe a bit wiser, I've become very aware of the gravity of this calling. None of us can do it alone. The time is <u>now</u> for the Church to become who she was made to be— the beautiful bride shining with love and anticipation as she awaits her groom. The love and glory of the Lord made visible in the earth.

The loving hands of a good Father reaching down to mend His broken children.

There are lovely things buried in the ugly places of this world. We, as Christians, need to be willing to search for them and see them as the hidden treasures that they are.

Anna and her willingness to give into what she heard God say. Jacob who said the F-word in his first prayer.

Beautiful gems!

The two people at our show in San Antonio. Donita, the charismatic powerhouse.

The kind Christians at the Rhema Bible Institute.

Matt and Aubrey in Waco, Texas. And Sam...

Our Japanese audience who didn't understand a word I said. The little pregnant drunk lady I met there in Osaka.

The endless lines of people who have waited to talk to me after a show for all these years.

Sparkling jewels—every single one of them!

201

Max, the atheist hooligan evangelist. Hannah, who escaped from her awful situation through the power of intercessory prayer.

Katie—who can now see. And Camille—who can now dance.

Sarah… Her smiles, her wisdom, and her 15 years of struggle against cancer.

Apostle Aaron and his leveling influence in my life. Our church family and the home they've given us.

Mike. Rory. The countless others that have been wounded in the senseless conflict between conservative culture and the homosexual community.

Precious pearls, handmade by God, who He wants in His kingdom. Each beautiful individual shining with an eternal beauty that only the hand of the Master Artist could have designed.

The French prostitutes. Everyone I met on Warped Tour.

Marcela and the staggering wounds she's carried. Matt and his funny French accent.

Could there be anything more lovely than these treasures?

What about the treasure inside you? Inside your friends, your family members, your enemies? Can you see it? It's there!

If God is seeking it in each of us (and He is), then we should be seeking it in each other.

I have a dream that somehow, of the millions of people who have heard our music, of the hundreds of thousands who have come to see us perform over the years, a handful might really hear what we've been shouting all along. My dream is that some heard more than music from us. That they found a hope that transcends their circumstances, a love that overcomes their fears and failures, and a faith that can stand firm in a world of ever-shifting standards. My dream is that out of our generation, the world might see a movement of men and women who are not concerned with fitting in, or meeting the shallow expectations of a godless culture, but who instead will stand as the light that confronts the darkness, the warmth that confronts the cold, and the peace that confronts the chaos.

And finally, I dream that through the story of our wild adventure of reckless abandon for the Gospel in the midst of an industry that largely opposes and dismisses it, many others might find the courage necessary to look also for the treasure hidden in the field. The passion to dig for the beauty created by God that lies buried under the rubble of sin and decay and pain that is all too common in this world. To seek out this lost generation. To search for and uncover the God-given beauty inside each person, the precious treasures hidden inside others.

After all, these are the *lovely things in ugly places*.

Made in the USA
San Bernardino, CA
19 June 2017